Praise for Jeffrey Hodges

Here are just a few of the   people and
coaches who have already   and books,
tapes, and performance enh

"A sensational read! Exce   *ok I have*
read for my sport, either phy
David Williams, Triathlete,

"This is a fantastic book and I recommend it to every sportsperson I know!"
Gareth Jones, Bodybuilding, Qld.

"Great book! It has already helped me win two Australian titles! I now need
to go further, and with your continued support I know this is possible"
Nadine Simpson, Tae-Kwon-Do, NSW. [Aust. middleweight champion]

"This training is the BEST! Added to your physical training you could do
anything."
Peter Buckworth, Rugby League, NSW.

"Your course was incredibly helpful, and has influenced my move to the next
stage in my career as a dancer. You have touched everybody in the class -
thank you!"
Adam Stone, Ballroom Dancing, NSW.

"Thankyou for your input to our Junior Surf Sports Camp. The comments
from those attending your vibrant sessions were very positive. I know the
benefits to all the young people you spoke to will not be restricted to just their
sporting achievements, but in their careers and privately as well."
Jim Fitzgerald, Regional Coaching & Development Officer, Surf Life
Saving Queensland.

"Outstanding book!"
Kellie Cuschieri, International Squash Competitor, ACT.

"What a superb book! As an athlete and coach I found it wonderfully
motivating."
Belinda Scowcroft, Track and Field Coach, NSW.

"I've been coaching for 8 years, and I've been to many seminars on mental training for elite athletes. The Sportsmind lecture which I and my elite athletes attended was the first that really went into depth .... My athletes trained harder the day after the lecture, and every session since. I highly recommend Jeffrey Hodges and his Sportsmind lectures are a must for anyone aspiring to more successful sports performance."
Sue Stevenson, Level 2 Table Tennis Coach, 1996 Australian Table Tennis Coach of the year.

"The SPORTSMIND correspondence course is interesting and informative, and applicable to elite referees and coaches, and our grass root accreditation and development programs."
Russell Trotter, Referees Manager, Australian Rugby Union.

"A joy to read - easy to understand, and so comprehensive. A great book!"
David Turner, Tennis, Qld.

"This is the most practical and well explained 'package' I have ever found."
Simon Bolte, Triathlete, NSW.

"The exercises do work That's all I wanted. Thanks "
Sean Power, Karate, NSW.

"After listening to your tape regularly over the past few weeks, I have really noticed a big difference in not only the way I am playing, but also the way I am thinking around the course. I feel much more confident, and very much in control of my feelings and emotions, and my concentration level is very high. Thank you very much for giving me what I feel is a competitive edge over my future opponents (and myself)."
Gregory Mack, Golf, NSW.

"Jeffrey Hodges presented a seminar to our top 35 players ... (it was) extremely positively received by the players. I have no hesitation in recommending him to any professional sporting organisation wishing to gain the competitive edge by tapping into the Sportsmind."
Bruce Hopkins, Training Director, Penrith Rugby League Football Club.

"The SPORTSMIND correspondence course is even better than I expected. I sincerely recommend it to any athlete or sports coach."
Ricky Budgen, Boxing Coach, Qld.

"This book has already given me the edge."
Malcolm Parker, Olympic Dinghy Sailing, Tas.

"Excellent! I've never come across a book of this standard before."
S. J. Doak, Tenpin Bowling, Qld.

"I thought you'd like to know about my latest successes - the umpires' award for Best on Court in State League B, and an invitation to join the Victorian Women's Cricket training squad. I'd like to thank you for your assistance in helping me achieve - or rather exceed - my goals set at the first seminar I attended last year. Without the seminars I wouldn't have been as focussed on achieving my goals, or have believed them achievable."
Kim Holmes, Netball and Cricket, Victoria.

"Just what I needed "
Cathy Wiegold, Long Distance Running, NSW.

"SPORTSMIND is the most amazing book I've ever read! Brilliant!"
Tony Kean, Triathlete, NSW.

"Through Sportsmind my mental game has improved out of sight, and I have already had some big wins because of it. Thank you !"
Craig Hayes, Table Tennis, Qld.

"Magic! The best I've found!"
Jennifer Rayment, Equestrian, Qld.

"Excellent book! A must read for any serious athlete or coaching body."
Dyson Martin, Martial Arts, Qld.

"I have played A grade rugby for five years and I feel that the mental aspect of my game can improve to take me to the next levels. Your book has particularly helped me to develop confidence in my play."
Andrew Johnson, Rugby, Qld.

"Thankyou for the helpful techniques I learned at the two workshops. I feel my attitude has changed so much since attending, now I am excited about what I can achieve and I think so many more people in my sport would benefit from the information you can give."
Kyanne Smith, ballroom dancer, NSW.

"A very educational book - even for a level 2 nationally accredited coach!"
Phillip Newton, Track and Field Coach, NSW.

"Inspiring!"
Marina Patan, Triathlete, NSW.

"This book has started me on the pathway of mental mastery on my way to Atlanta. Thankyou!"
Liane Fenwick, Beach Volleyball Olympian, NSW.

"The areas Jeff has covered with the athletes are:
  - Positive Motivation and Sports Goals
  - Positive Self Image and Confidence
  - Concentration and Anxiety Management
  - Visualisation
These areas have been a great help to my athletes in attaining their goals, and are very helpful to the boys in other areas beside sport. Jeff has terrific rapport with teenagers who respond well to his work. He is very professional and to the point without going over the top. I have been very happy with the workshops Jeff has run, and I would recommend him to any coach involved with teenagers."
John Bowes, Director of Rowing, St. Joseph's College.

"Totally awesome book! Just brilliant!"
Beneta Popovic, Badminton, NSW.

"Your clinic was the best course I've ever done!"
Todd Bowden, squash player, NSW.

"Very personable. Excellent content. GREAT!"
Shelley Oates, Olympic Kayaker, NSW.

"Sportsmind is a tremendous read. The information and techniques are easy to use and improve the performance of both athletes and sports trainers alike. It was timely and helped me enormously."
Colin Richardson, Gridiron Coach, NSW.

"I've driven a total of 930 kilometres over four days to be at these Sportsmind workshops, and it's been worth every kilometre!"
Harold McNair, Soccer coach, Vic.

"Wonderful concepts, with enormous potential application particularly with junior sports people."
Theo Trovas, Basketball, Qld.

"I found your tape on Concentration just terrific!"
Barbara Armytage, Bowls, NSW.

"Guess what! In the USA I won a $25,000 Challenger event which bumped my ranking up about 100 places. I'm now ranked 237 in the world (my career best so far) and I can only get better as I can now get into bigger tournaments. I just wanted to share this good news with you since you've helped me so much in the past. Thanks for all your help!"
Gail Biggs, Tennis, Qld.

"Terrific! I'm really fired up to succeed!"
Zita van de Walle, Rowing, NSW.

"I appreciated the presentation, and extremely well delivered. Content was great - even my twelve year old son said it was a fantastic learning experience. Your 'positive bubble' exercise is a life changing concept!"
Joel and Richard Siegersma, Baseball, NSW.

"Visualisation really works! After attending Jeffrey's Sportsmind seminar, instead of extra training I lay on a beach visualising, and improved dramatically to win the Champion Lady Rider at Royal Melbourne Show! Way to go!"
Sally McPherson, Dressage, Vic.

"Visualisation, mental rehearsal and positive mental attitude ..... I took what I learned at the Sportsmind workshops and applied it through our recent netball finals, and was awarded best on court! Thanks Jeff!"
Robyn Forte, Netball, Vic.

"The three sessions were very valuable for our girls and were focused on the needs of our players - the practical techniques led straight to their sporting needs to enhance their performance. I was impressed with the input and presentation and its relativity to our Netball players. Well done!"
Michelle White, Coaching Convenor, Northern Beaches Netball, NSW.

See inside the back cover for more comments ......

Acknowledgments

The following individuals have provided sources of inspiration,
encouragement, and assistance without which this book
would not have been possible.
Thankyou to you all :

First and foremost to my wife Susan, and children Benjamin and Lauren, whose patience and sacrifices over the past six and a half years as I have established *Sportsmind* as the pre-eminent mental and emotional training program for sportspeople in Australia, have been truly monumental.

Terry McClendon and Kasrynne Huolohan, my teachers and colleagues in NLP, provided invaluable inspiration, encouragement and opportunities for me to learn and develop my NLP and Ericksonian Hypnosis skills over the past *fifteen years*, without which neither this book, nor *Sportsmind*, would exist. Thanks also to the inspirational John Syer and Chris Connolly - who were responsible for starting me on this path in the first place - way back in 1980, at Findhorn in Scotland! Is it really *18 years* since I left?

Significant others to thank are Graham Bird and David ('Doc') Wescombe-Down, my academic supervisors whose wisdom, experience and assistance were greatly valued, and who ably guided me through to the successful completion of my M.Sc.(Hons) degree in 1997; Lyn Larsen, Rachelle Adam, Bill Lyon, Leoni Baldwin, Mark Robson, Shannon Gaffney, Katrina Haddrill, and Diane Hay from the NSW Dept. of Sport & Recreation, whose assistance and organisational skills made the field-work component of my research possible, and who provided their local sporting communities with the opportunity of participating in *Sportsmind* workshops; the numerous journalists from around Australia who took the time to interview me about the *Sportsmind* project - particularly those from the ABC who were consistently supportive throughout the entire six and a half years, and continue to be so; the staff and my fellow students in Social Ecology who provided so much intellectual stimulation and support at residential programs, particular thanks to Monika Gaede, John Clarke, John Cameron, Rob Ebsary, Kay Fielden, Peter Melser, Lesley Kuhn-White, Hinton Lowe, Kalevi Kopra. Thanks too to Chris and Jules Collingwood for their friendship and support and for bringing John Grinder to Australia - what an experience! Finally, thanks to Melinda Rene, of Rene Graphics, for the wonderful cover design.

CHAMPION THOUGHTS, CHAMPION FEELINGS

Use the Strategies of Champions to be More Successful in <u>Your</u> Life!

Jeffrey D. Hodges B.Sc.(AES) M.Sc.(Hons)

SPORTSMIND INTERNATIONAL INSTITUTE FOR HUMAN PERFORMANCE RESEARCH

Other Books by Jeffrey Hodges

Harvesting the Suburbs [1985]
Natural Gardening & Farming in Australia [1989]
Water Efficient Gardening (with J. Archer & B. Le Hunt) [1993]
The Natural Gardener (Editor) [1995]

Learn Faster, Now! [1992]
Sportsmind [1993]

10% of the proceeds from sales of all *Sportsmind* products go to the Men of the Trees, *Tree Farm Project* - to plant viable crop trees in degraded rural areas of Australia. Since 1985 this money has provided *just over $ 53,000.00* for this worthwhile project.
Thankyou for supporting tree planting
in Australia with your purchase of *Sportsmind* products.

Copyright :   Jeffrey D. Hodges June, 1998.
This work is copyright. All rights reserved. No part of this publication may be reproduced, stored or transmitted in any form or by any means whatsoever without written permission of the publisher:

SPORTSMIND INTERNATIONAL INSTITUTE
FOR HUMAN PERFORMANCE RESEARCH
77 FLAXTON MILL ROAD FLAXTON. QLD. 4560.

National Library of Australia Cataloguing-in-Publication data :

Hodges, Jeffrey.
Champion thoughts, champion feelings : use the strategies of champions to be more successful in your life.

Bibliography.
ISBN 0 9590124 4 3

1. Success - Handbooks, manuals, etc. 2. Neurolinguistic programming. I. Title.

158

About Jeffrey Hodges

Jeffrey Hodges is a performance consultant to elite athletes, sporting teams and corporate clients. He is the author of the widely acclaimed *"Sportsmind - An Athlete's Guide to Superperformance Through Mental & Emotional Training"*; creator of the *Sportsmind* performance enhancement workshops and audio tapes; and Director of the *Sportsmind Institute for Human Performance Research.*

He is a NLP *Master Practitioner* and *Associate Trainer*, and his landmark M.Sc.(Hons) thesis involving 893 athletes from over thirty different sports established the effectiveness of NLP techniques for mental skills training in sport.

His *Sportsmind* programs have been endorsed by the NSW Dept Sport & Recreation, and recommended by top sportsclubs and successful athletes. He has presented workshops to thousands of sportspeople throughout Australia, to professional sports clubs, and for corporate clients. Jeffrey has competed in many sports, notably Volleyball, Squash, Soccer and Golf. He currently trains in Aikido, holds a grade of 1st Kyu (brown belt), and expects to attain his black belt by the end of 1998.

Some of his clients to date include :
Australian Rugby Union; St. Joseph's College; Woodlands Golf Club; Financial Institutions Remuneration Group (FIRG); Societe Generale; Lend Lease; Qld. Swimming; Network for Fitness Professionals; North Sydney and Penrith Rugby League Clubs; Qld. Athletics Assn; NSW Netball Assn; Northern Inland Academy of Sport; Victorian Soaring Assn; Orange Agricultural College Equestrian School; Qld and NSW Departments of Sport and Recreation; and the RAAF.

Jeffrey Hodges B.Sc.(AES) M.Sc.(Hons) AIMM
Master Practitioner N.L.P. & Ericksonian Hypnosis

CONTENTS

"You are a champion because you acknowledge the help of others – knowing you could never have done it alone."

CHAPTER 1 :

MODELLING EXCELLENCE

INTRODUCTION

Champions.......

We've all watched and admired them at the Olympics, the NBA playoffs, the World Cup, the World Series, Wimbledon, the US Masters Golf, the Superbowl, or the Ashes Tests.

Whether they be a Pete Sampras, a Michael Jordan, a Pele, a Susie O'Neill, a Greg Norman, a Carl Lewis, a Greg Le Mond, a Stefi Graf, a Michael Johnson, a Mark Spitz, a Heather Mackay, a Kieran Perkins, a Joe Montana, a Tiger Woods, a Martina Hingis, or a Sir Donald Bradman, despite their very different 'personalities', there are characterising traits common to them all.

Champion traits.

They all share *Champion thoughts, Champion feelings.*

THOUGHTS AND FEELINGS

Something sets these champions apart from everyone else - what is it that makes them so apparently different from the 'average' person? What is it that enables them to succeed at the highest level, under sustained pressure and competition so consistently?

It can be recognised that everything you do in the external world, every behaviour, every action, and every performance, has to *first* happen internally - within your mind and emotions. *Your thoughts and feelings affect your performance*, and every behaviour - whether it be getting nervous before a ten foot putt to win the Club Championship; being energised and enthusiastic before the grand final; or acting despondent because your partner left you - *has to first happen in your head* before it happens 'out there'.

Every performance has to first happen *internally* - in your mind and emotions.

The structure of your internal thoughts and feelings then, produces all the results in your life - be they success or failure; prosperity or poverty; health or illness.

Understanding this simple principle, we can re-phrase the above question about what makes a champion into :

* "What do *Champions* do in their mind and with their emotions that allows them to perform outstandingly, time and time again?"

* "What are the *Champion thoughts* and *Champion feelings* that allow them to perform so well?"

More importantly, can these *Champion thoughts* and *Champion feelings* be taught to others - to help them enhance their personal performances as a student, a business leader, a teacher, a parent, and in their sport? The answer is an emphatic YES!! Anyone can learn how to think and feel like a champion, and significantly enhance their life.

Your thoughts and feelings affect your performance -
think and *feel* **like a Champion to improve your life.**

The ideas in this book have been gleaned from my study of the *Champion* thoughts, feelings and behaviours of successful athletes, top business leaders, superb educators, powerful motivators, excellent communicators, and inspirational achievers from around the world.

You may have already heard about some of the ideas from people such as Anthony Robbins, Jack Canfield, Jim Rohn, Maxwell Maltz, Denis Waitley, Richard Bandler, Milton Erickson, John Grinder, and others, and I sincerely acknowledge the positive influence that all these people have made toward this book.

However, ideas are only useful if they are *put into action*. Ideas without action just lead to daydreams and delusions. I've found that people read an inspirational book, but don't put into practice the ideas they just read - and so nothing much changes for them.

Consequently, when I began my work researching and writing about the success strategies of top athletes, I wanted to design a program that would encourage people to implement the ideas in their lives. I also wanted to ensure that everything I wrote about *worked*, in practice, with real life situations.

THE SPORTSMIND PROJECT :
MODELLING EXCELLENCE

This was how the *Sportsmind* research project and performance enhancement workshops came about. *Sportsmind* was my first book on the *mental* success strategies of top sportspeople, and I implemented an extensive research project involving 893 athletes and coaches from over thirty different sports, to demonstrate that *anyone* could significantly enhance their sports performances simply by developing the seven skills of the *Sportsmind* :

* **Positive Motivation**
* **Goal Setting**
* **Concentration**
* **Positive Mental Attitude**
* **Positive Self Concept**
* **Visualisation.**

My research comprised a five year scientific study of the effectiveness of the *Sportsmind* material, conducted in conjunction with the University of Western Sydney, and identified significant performance enhancements from attendance at *Sportsmind* workshops.

On average, participants noted that the *Sportsmind workshops improved their performances between 35 - 44%.* Even more definitive results were obtained with seven case study athletes who attended all four one-day *Sportsmind* training workshops. The results of these case studies found, on average, that participants believed that the *Sportsmind workshops had improved their sports performances by 47.1%.* Further, they all identified significant *objective* improvements, such as increase in grade of play, awards, competition victories, and so on.

It's been over seven years since I began that research, and five years since I first published the *Sportsmind* book, and over that time I've received hundreds of letters from sportspeople about how the *Sportsmind* ideas have benefited them in their training and competition. During this time I've also worked with over 3,000 sportspeople personally, and conducted more than 200 *Sportsmind* workshops and lectures all over Australia.

The *Sportsmind* book has become a best seller, and been widely acclaimed throughout the sporting community. However, when I wrote *Sportsmind* I wanted it to be read by *everyone*, not just sportspeople, because the seven 'success' skills of the sports mind apply just as much to business, or sales, or education, or the performing arts as they do to sports performance.

The skills of the *Sportsmind* apply just as much to business, education, or the performing arts as to sport.

So while this new book still has a strong sports orientation, please recognise that all the ideas are equally applicable to improving your results at school or university study, for increasing your financial income, for advancing in your career or business, for becoming a better speaker and for developing better relationships.

I hope you've picked it up to improve your whole life, and not just your sports performances.

To assist you, I've put this book together in a way that's different from all the other 'self-help' and motivational books I've seen. First, as in *Sportsmind*, you will notice that there are some very practical tools and exercises that you can use right from the first chapter to make an immediate positive impact on your life.

Secondly, I've structured each chapter so that it covers a general concept, (eg. emotions), with an explanation of the ideas I want to present; I then describe a performance enhancement technique, usually with an example of a case study athlete I've worked with showing how the technique has benefited them; and finally there's an exercise for you to do to implement the technique on yourself.

Please, don't just be inspired, or have an amazing 'realisation' as you read this book. Inspiration without action is a missed opportunity. 'Realisation' without sobriety leads to shallow emotional outbursts, but little real change.

Do take the steps necessary to make the *Champion* thoughts and feelings in this book your own.

Inspiration without action is a missed opportunity.

One of the main reasons for undertaking the *Sportsmind* research project was to educate athletes and coaches about the importance of mental and emotional training, particularly in light of the failure of many sport 'psychology' practitioners to provide easily understood concepts and practical techniques for athletes to use.

Unfortunately, sport 'psychology' for many sportspeople and coaches is still, in the words of one athlete, "*a load of rubbish*" - being too complex and theoretical that it's no wonder most sportspeople have little time for it. *Current sport psychology suffers from too much psychology, and not enough sport!*

I hope through my Masters thesis and the phenomenal results I've achieved with the *Sportsmind* research project, and in this book, to have a positive influence and provide more *practical* ideas.

THE FAILURE OF SPORT 'PSYCHOLOGY'

In my opinion, the failing in current sport psychology is that it uses an archaic approach to human behaviour and performance, based on psychological profiles, personality analyses, and dubious questionnaires and tests with questionable veracity and usefulness - and is far removed from the sweat and effort of the playing field, and totally out of touch with the needs of real sportspeople.

Current sport psychology suffers from too much psychology, and not enough sport!

In the early years of sports psychology, one of the primary goals was to identify the 'psychological profile' of a champion athlete - the aim being to use such a profile in the recruitment and selection of potentially 'talented' players. However, this was discredited *because no consistent profiles were ever identified*!

Despite this obvious failure of 'personality' based approaches, the current thinking in sport psychology is that perhaps the problem wasn't that the concept of looking for profiles was wrong, but rather that the *tools* they were using were inadequate: they used personality tests from general psychology but these didn't detect relevant differences because they weren't designed to do so! [What's that old saying about a poor workman blaming his tools?]

Now there is a plethora of 'sport-specific psychological tests' such as: "Test of Attentional and Interpersonal Style (TAIS)", "Sport Competition Anxiety Test (SCAT)", "Competitive State Anxiety Inventory-2 (CSAI-2)", and "Profile of Mood States (POMS)". Is it any wonder that most sports people have little understanding of, or desire to understand, current sport psychology!

I believe such personality approaches will continue to prove fruitless, because the concept of the 'personality' is too undefined, and existing models, (and foreseeable future developments in this field), are inadequate to the task - and rarely equal to an experienced coach's 'gut feeling' and subjective judgements for the identification and selection of potentially 'talented' players.

Further, I don't believe that a particular personality is what makes for a successful sportsperson - and this is rather obvious when one considers the widely variant 'personalities' of the existing cadre of elite level athletes across the sporting continuum.

Nor, in my opinion, is it as some would suggest, particular personal *attributes* that make a champion. Such tends to suggest that sporting 'success' traits are inherently genetic in nature - you've either got 'it' or you haven't got 'it'; whatever 'it' is.

Anyone can be trained to become a talented player by using successful thinking and feeling *strategies*.

Rather, I suggest that basically *anyone* can be trained to become a talented player by identifying the successful *sports strategies* of a given sport, (as contrasted to personal attributes), and teaching them these success strategies. *Anyone* despite their 'personality' (if such a thing exists at all, which I doubt), can adopt and make use of a particular thinking and feeling *success strategy*.

So I believe the correct approach is not to spend time assessing the *individual* 'personality' attributes of athletes, but rather to concentrate attention and training on such *general* behavioural success strategies. Identify these, and then develop training programs to teach them to all athletes and coaches.

FROM SPORT 'PSYCHOLOGY' TO SPORTS NLP !

The identification of, and training in, such behavioural success strategies is the purlieu of the field of Neuro-Linguistic Programming - or NLP. Consequently, this is not a book on sport 'psychology', but rather a book on *practical performance enhancement* by taking charge of your thoughts and feelings with the use of NLP - not just another 'personality' profiling system!

Probably the greatest failing of sport psychology, and psychology in general, is it's continued refusal to accept the advances made in human performance enhancement through the field of NLP.

NLP is a powerful new human performance technology, that has provided elegant tools for improving human performance in the areas of management, education, sales and counselling. Essentially, NLP is about *modelling excellence* - identifying the *cognitive strategies* and *emotional states* that provide the means by which anyone achieves success in any endeavour.

NLP is about *modelling excellence*.

It surprises me that the field of sports psychology, (which is supposedly concerned with peak performance), has not embraced these extremely powerful and practical techniques of NLP. For instance, the first published work on NLP, which coined the term, was *The Structure of Magic* published in 1975, and this has been followed by a plethora of excellent books, many of which have become classics in the field: *Frogs Into Princes (1979); Reframing (1980); Using Your Brain for a Change (1985); Change Your Mind and Keep the Change (1987); Heart of the Mind (1989); Beliefs (1990)* and *Core Transformations (1993).*

However in the over twenty years now since the advent of NLP, there has been little investigation into the applications of this revolutionary behavioural technology to sports psychology and psychological skills training in sport. [A recent search of *Dissertation Abstracts* listed only *eight items on NLP*, none of which related to sports applications!]

Psychological researchers question the validity of some of the claims of NLP practitioners, and doubt some aspects of the NLP model - notably, the relationship between eye movements and sensory system usage; personal sensory system preference; and some of the presuppositions of the NLP model of - and it is true that there is little support in the existing scientific literature for the NLP theories which have been tested scientifically.

Research into NLP receives little funding or intellectual support at universities.

However, I think it is obvious that the current psychological hierarchy is far from 'objective' in its investigations of NLP, and a strong case can be argued that 'research' on NLP is *actively discouraged* by academic supervisors at universities, and therefore it receives little funding or intellectual support. Secondly, those aspects of the NLP model which *have* been investigated have, in my opinion, been among the *least* practically useful techniques - particularly from a sports perspective - and because of their controversial nature have attracted attention away from more credible techniques. Here I specifically refer to the NLP behavioural excellence modelling techniques mentioned earlier that have been used to initiate positive generative change in individuals, (as compared to remedial change), many of which have only been developed in the last five to ten years.

Because many of these generative NLP techniques have only been developed quite recently, very little quality research has been undertaken, particularly in the sports applications of NLP. It seems very strange that there are so few published articles or papers on NLP, and that it barely makes a mention in any psychology or sport psychology conferences. Perhaps it is an unfortunate truth that, as Connirae and Steve Andreas note in their introduction to Richard Bandler's (1985) *'Using Your Brain for a Change'*, it appears that *incompetence is rewarded in the field of psychology!*

It appears that incompetence is rewarded in the field of psychology!

Isn't it true that, always, whenever a revolutionary innovation occurs in business, computing, communications technology, and so on, manufacturers around the world all scramble to make immediate use of the new ideas? If they didn't, their competitors would put them out of business! For instance, just think of the huge changes that have occurred in telecommunications or computing in just the past five years!

However, in psychology, people seem to get paid *more* if they take longer to solve a problem! Andreas suggests that since incompetence is rewarded, new and better methods take a lot longer to become part of the mainstream in psychology.

Likewise, Richard Bandler, one of the designers of NLP, makes some very pertinent comments about the limitations of the field of psychology, suggesting that one of the reasons for the failure of psychology to provide quick effective methods for change, is that psychology mostly studies *broken* people.

It then attempts to use that as a basis for teaching people how to be healthy, happy and successful! Which, as he rightly suggests, is a bit like studying the smashed up cars at the wreckers to figure out how to build a high performance sports car!

I think one of the pitfalls for manypracticing sports psychologists, particularly in Australia, is that they have been trained as psychologist *first*, and sports coaches or motivators second, and they thus suffer from the same psychological malaises described so eloquently by Richard Bandler above. There is a huge inertia in the field, and a reluctance to try new ideas; particularly ideas which have not been generated by their own ranks.

Sport psychology suffers from the same malaises as general psychology.

The other point to make is that NLP is the study of *subjective reality* - it studies the success strategies of people who are excelling at something, be it counselling, sport, sales, or whatever. NLP models *what works* - surely that needs some recognition!

For instance, most of the actual practical processes and techniques used in NLP have been drawn from the therapeutic repertoires of superb psychotherapists such as Virginia Satir, Milton Erickson and Fritz Perls - all of whom have been giants in their fields, and whose therapeutic interventions have proved effective, and been thoroughly substantiated.

So, in the work done using Neuro-Linguistic Programming in psychotherapy, there has been considerable success in effecting fast and lasting behavioural changes for maladaptive behavioural problems from phobias, to compulsive and addictive behaviours.

More recent work in Neuro-Linguistic Programming has progressed from this type of 'remedial' problem solving, to effecting *generative behavioural excellence*, ie. assisting people to do *better* what they already do well.

NLP fosters *generative behavioural excellence*.

As a consequence, I believe the NLP model has enormous potential for sports application - not only in helping sportspeople overcome 'negative' behaviours such as lapses in concentration, lack of motivation, loss of confidence, nervousness, and so on, but more importantly in effecting *generative behavioural excellence* - assisting sportspeople to do *better* what they already do well, and in teaching the successful mental strategies and behavioural capabilities of elite sportspeople to others.

It is these generative techniques which form the basis for many of the techniques in this book. In particular, I've identified and utilised three building blocks of NLP that are of significant use in sports applications, and which are described in detail in later chapters: *Strategies, Anchoring States,* and *Submodality Shifts.*

The *Sportsmind* book provided the first psychological skills training program to include a range of NLP techniques designed for sports applications, and it is this focus on NLP methods that has made the *Sportsmind* program so successful.

Sportsmind was the first NLP program designed for sports performance.

Since NLP techniques utilise verifiable, sensory based descriptions of an individual's *subjective experience*, and practical tools and specific techniques for improving motivation, persistence and performance, (in contrast to the ambiguous personality tests and outdated psychological theories of traditional sport psychology), in my opinion NLP techniques will become the benchmark for both performance enhancement programs for competitive athletes, and behavioural change approaches for health and fitness clients, in the future.

> **NLP techniques utilise verifiable, sensory based descriptions of an individual's subjective experience, and *practical* tools for improving performance.**

These specific NLP concepts and techniques, (eg. 'Submodalities', 'Time Lines', 'Circle of Excellence', 'Strategies', 'Anchoring', 'Belief Change', 'Perceptual Shifts', and so on), are discussed in detail in the following chapters and in the *Sportsmind* book.

Consequently, this is a book specifically on the *practical applications of NLP* - and how to use the techniques to enhance your performance both in your sport, and elsewhere in your life.

It leads on from the ideas I presented in *Sportsmind*, so if you haven't yet read *Sportsmind*, I recommend that you do so.

> **NLP techniques will provide the benchmark for performance enhancement programs for all competitive athletes in future.**

UNDERSTANDING THE NLP APPROACH

Thus t

NLP originated from the work of Richard Ba
Grinder when they pooled their considerable tal
and *model* the counselling strategies and therape
employed by superb psychotherapists such as Fritz Perls, Milton
Erickson, and Virginia Satir. What resulted was an effective
model not only of excellence in counselling, but also a unique
model of human behaviour, *and a specific technology of human
behavioural modelling and behavioural change*, based on a
specific theory of the structure of human subjective experience.

Essentially the NLP theory of behaviour suggests that behaviour
is a consequence of mental processes, or strategies, and that these
strategies have an identifiable structure and content.

**Behaviour is a consequence of mental processing
strategies with an identifiable structure and content.**

Human cognitions can take the form of one of five sensory
components - *visual, auditory, kinaesthetic, olfactory and
gustatory*, (that is, we can *see* something in our mind; we can
hear something or talk to ourselves; we can *feel* things internally;
and we can experience *smells* and *tastes* mentally), and these
specific mental *representations* of experience link together to
establish behavioural strategies, which then direct our behaviour.

For example, take a simple decision making strategy. In order to
make a decision about something, (for instance about buying a
new car or a new dress), an individual may first *picture* it in their
mind, then *talk* to themselves about it, then get a *feeling* about
what to do, and then act upon the decision.

...e decision making strategy can be represented as :

V ---> A ---> K ----> Decision

Hence, *since any and every behaviour can be usefully represented as a sequence of identifiable sensory based steps, these steps can be learned, and reproduced, to effect a similar behavioural outcome.* Further, maladaptive behaviours, (for example pre-performance anxiety, unconfidence, etc.), can be reduced to their component parts, and specific interventions designed to ameliorate the problem, quickly and effectively.

Every behaviour can be represented as a sequence of identifiable sensory based steps.

This is precisely where NLP differs from traditional 'psychology' - by providing *verifiable, sensory based descriptions* of an individual's subjective experience, and practical tools and specific techniques for enhancing that experience. NLP has a range of fresh, innovative ideas and practical tools to effect positive behavioural change, while traditional psychology can only offer outdated theories and unverifiable concepts.

NLP provides verifiable, sensory based descriptions of subjective experience.

I like to define NLP as the study of how the way we think affects our behaviour and performance. Using NLP you can learn how to use your thoughts and feelings in ways that will enhance your communication and performance in all areas of your life.

Chris and Jules Collingwood, in their excellent book, *Personal Strategies for Life* (1995), define NLP in this way:

"If Neuro-Linguistic Programming is the study of the structure of subjective experience, and the study of how we know what we know, then it is an epistemology. It can also be described as a methodology, or a meta-model. Using NLP, we can isolate and describe patterns of thinking and awareness as used by real people who act in the world with excellence. This is the art of modelling, or replicating talent.

Strictly speaking modelling can be applied to any skill at any level ...... By studying the patterns of thinking underlying behaviour and capabilities, desired behaviour and capabilities can be replicated and transferred. As a result, the skills and capabilities of the best performers in a particular line of work can be described in a replicable form and transferred to others who want to operate at high levels of excellence. ....

The first descriptions the originators of NLP created came from three of the most effective psychotherapists of the time. Subsequently, in its early days, many people thought that NLP was a communication system for doing therapy. Later, after certain capabilities were modelled from the business world, a number of applications developed. These included business communications, negotiation skills, meeting management, presentation / speaking techniques and sales training. As a result, another misconception arose, to the effect that NLP was something to do with effective selling or public speaking.

In fact the descriptions of various capabilities developed by Neuro-linguistic programmers are the output of the NLP methodology, skilfully applied, not the methodology itself." (p10)

In other words, NLP is a human performance and behavioural change technology based on *modelling excellence* - identifying the motivation and thinking strategies of highly successful people, and providing practical tools for teaching these to others.

NLP is not simply a set of techniques, or even a particular methodology.

However, it should be recognised that NLP is not simply a set of techniques, nor just a particular methodology. The practice of NLP involves an acceptance of the following four principles:
1. A 'no-limits, possibility' attitude;
2. An outcome oriented methodology;
3. A large range of sensory-based, change techniques;
4. Understanding of a set of presuppositions of the NLP approach to human behaviour and personal change.

To conclude this chapter, I want to spend a little time explaining each of these four principles of the practice of NLP in detail, since the chapters that follow will provide the specific NLP tools, and to use the tools effectively you will want to also understand the principles behind their application.

1. A 'No-Limits, Possibility' Attitude
An essential ingredient in the practice of NLP is a personal attitude and belief held by the NLP practitioner that *anything is possible*; that human beings are truly amazing, and that *what one person can do, anyone else can also learn to do.*

To the NLP practitioner, *anything is possible!*

Another way of putting this is to say that NLP practitioners hold a belief that there are no limits to human possibility; that nothing is 'impossible' - except to those who believe so! Not that this is necessarily true, but that if one *acts as if it is true*, then phenomenal things can happen!

This kind of attitude is best illustrated by the example of Robert Dilts, one of the significant contributors to the NLP model in recent years. When his mother was diagnosed with a recurrence of breast cancer, (that had metastasised to her skull, spine, ribs and pelvis), she was given no hope by the medical fraternity - yet Robert approached this 'impossible' situation with his belief that anything is possible, and used all his NLP skills to help her change her beliefs about health and healing.

Without any treatment, other than NLP, she made a full recovery from cancer!

Without chemotherapy, radiation therapy or any other traditional treatment she made a full recovery, with no further cancer symptoms, and has maintained excellent health for years since!

Such stories are commonplace in the NLP literature, with people being healed of illnesses from cancer to back pain; individuals overcoming phobias they have suffered with for years, in just one short NLP session; people recovering from horrific accidents and crippling injuries to lead normal active lives again; athletes no longer suffering from pre-performance anxiety, and playing way beyond previous performance standards; 'ordinary' people doing extraordinary things they never thought possible for them, stretching their boundaries and testing their physical, emotional and mental limits to achieve 'impossible' dreams.

However, it's not only one's personal beliefs that are important in NLP - the NLP practitioner also has a special attitude toward their clients. It could be said that traditional psychology focuses on, and treats 'problems', and so people are seen to be full of pathological problems which must be overcome.

The NLP practitioner on the other hand, has a *solution focus* and utilises an approach of *client education and learning*, rather than 'problem solving'. People are not full of pathological problems, but are simply using poor strategies which need to be reprogrammed.

NLP seeks to *educate* rather than solve 'problems'.

This attitude is so important, particularly when dealing with sports people. Sportspeople are always pushing their boundaries and teasing the edges of their capabilities - this is what is so inspiring about playing and watching sport! So when dealing with an athlete, it's useful to take the attitude that they are not someone with 'problems' to fix - for example, "I've lost my motivation", or "I have lapses in concentration", or "I'm unconfident when I play away games", or whatever - but rather as someone who is at a certain level of competency who desires to be even better.

Thus the process changes from a 'problem' focus; from "What's *wrong* with me?" and trying to 'fix' it, to one of simple education. Simply learning some new skills and techniques which enable them to move from where they are to where they want to be.

NLP takes you from where you are, to where you want to be.

2. An Outcome Oriented Methodology

This leads on to the next NLP principle - that of an outcome oriented methodology. Basically this means that someone has a 'present state' in which they experience some sort of unwanted, negative behaviour or feeling, and want to change to a 'desired state' in which they have a more positive behaviour or feeling.

Traditional psychotherapy would attempt to analyse the problem state, determine why, where and when it came about, and through this 'understanding' supposedly assist the client - after months, or even years of therapy!

NLP on the other hand *focuses on the desired outcome* the client wants, and provides resources to assist them to get there. Provided you can achieve the desired state, and maintain it consistently, it is irrelevant, and a waste of time and effort to consider when, where, and why the problem originated!

NLP focuses on the *desired outcome* and provides resources to get there.

This principle of establishing a desired outcome with clients is extremely useful, because in unresourceful situations most people focus on their problem, whatever it may be, forgetting the simple truism that *your unconscious resources follow your focus.* Focus on a problem and you give it power, and often make it worse!

However by the simple act of establishing a desired outcome for someone, you've already started a change process in motion, because the brain will automatically and unconsciously seek out a means of achieving it. *Focus on the solution, and you empower yourself to find a way to achieve it!*

You may recall that in *Sportsmind* I spoke about one of the most important functions of the non-conscious self - that of upholding the 'reality' of a person's self image. You automatically and unconsciously act out 'yourself' - you don't have to think about it, or try to remember who you are; you're just you!

The mechanism by which this works is known as the Reticular Activating System (RAS), which is a part of the brain that acts like a kind of filter - blocking out information that is not currently 'relevant' or 'true' to the existing self image and goals of an individual. In addition, once a specific goal or outcome is clearly identified, this Reticular Activating System goes to work to actively seek out appropriate information, ideas, and resources, and it will automatically organise your behaviour to achieve it.

> **Once you clearly identify a desired outcome or goal, the RAS in your brain organises your behaviour to achieve it.**

This is readily observable in all aspects of our life. For instance, if you've ever built a house, and are at the stage of choosing a certain colour and style of brick, you will find yourself automatically noticing the bricks on the houses in your neighbourhood, and as you drive to work - whereas previous to your decision to look at bricks, you probably never even noticed the houses in your area, let alone what kind of bricks they had!

The human brain is a naturally goal seeking, cybernetic 'mechanism', and as soon as you clearly identify a target, your brain is unconsciously finding ways to get you there. I'll be talking more about this important principle in chapter 3, and you can understand the importance of a clear, desired outcome now.

3. A Large Range of Sensory-Based, Change Techniques

Probably the single most characterising trait of NLP that distinguishes it from other psychological models and approaches, is its demanding of practitioners to develop a finely tuned set of observation skills to be able to 'calibrate' the internal processing strategies and emotional states of clients, so as to 'track' them through the change process from problem state to desired state.

These calibration skills are also used to substantiate - in unambiguous, sensory based terms - that the client *has actually achieved the desired change in behaviour or feeling state.*

NLP practitioners use a finely tuned set of observation skills to be able to 'calibrate' that the client has actually achieved desired changes.

This is in marked contrast to other psychological models which use theoretical concepts to guide their interventions, and have few verifiable means, if any, to identify the success, or not, of their work!

This is one of the reason why NLP training cannot be properly taught from just a book or set of tapes - however comprehensive and well produced such materials are. [Even *this* book, which is the most comprehensive Sports-NLP book yet written, can only provide you with a basic understanding of the principles and techniques of NLP] *NLP practitioners must learn in an apprenticeship format, and under the strict supervision of internationally recognised and accredited NLP trainers, these essential observation and calibration skills of NLP.* [More information on NLP Practitioner Training courses is provided in the back of this book]

In addition to the above mentioned observation and calibration skills, NLP practitioners have at their disposal a very large range of proven effective behavioural and emotional change techniques, developed over the past twenty years.

Essentially, any 'problem' state takes one of two possible forms: either the person wants to change some kind of *behaviour*, (eg. stop smoking; no longer procrastinate; don't eat junk food; be a better parent; etc.); or they want to change how they *feel*, (eg. feel confident and relaxed instead of nervous before big matches; feel more aggressive and 'killer instinct' when winning; feel more motivated to train; feel comfortable making sales calls to potential customers; let go of disappointment about a loss or failure; etc.)

A skilled NLP practitioner will tailor a change process to suit individual needs.

NLP provides specific tools to work with both of these forms of problem states - and a skilled practitioner will tailor a change process to suit an individual's needs, and even design a new intervention technique if required. These techniques are all client-centred, empowering the client with the means to change negative and limiting beliefs; replace negative emotions and feelings with positive ones; identify and achieve desired goals; improve their interpersonal communication skills; get out of 'stuck' states; and generally take charge of their own thoughts and feelings.

4. Understanding of a set of presuppositions of the NLP
   approach to human behaviour

The final NLP principle is a list of basic presuppositions of the NLP model, about human behaviour and personal change, and which provides an insight into understanding the NLP approach.

The following list is modified after one provided by Chris and Jules Collingwood in *Personal Strategies for Life*, (1995).

"* *The map is not the territory. There is difference between the actual world and that which we perceive.*

* *Everyone has a unique model of the world distorted, generalised, and deleted in infinitely variable combinations.*

* *People always make the best choices available to them, given their unique model of the world, and their situation.*

* *There is a solution (a desirable outcome) to every problem.*

* *Everyone has everything they need to solve their problems.*

* *There is a distinction between a person and their behaviour. Behaviour is something a person does, not who they are.*

* *The behaviour a person exhibits is separate from the intention of that behaviour. The intention is always assumed to be positive. Intention comes from the individual's unique model of the world which is different from that of the recipient.*

* *The meaning of a communication is the response it elicits. The recipient responds to the message as they perceive it.*

* *In interactions between people, the person with the most flexibility and variation of behaviour controls the interaction.*

* *Memory and imagination use the same neurological circuits and potentially have the same impact.*

* *Knowledge, thought, memory and imagination are the result of sequences and combinations of representational systems recalled from personal history, constructed from imagination and experienced directly from the environment.*

* *Mind and body are part of the same cybernetic structure and anything which alters one part of the system affects the rest.*

* *If what you're doing isn't working, do something different.*

* *Change work is profound when done in all systems. "* (p. 11)

In the following chapters you will learn the NLP techniques to assist yourself and others to achieve excellence.

"You are a champion because you aim high — knowing that the quality of the goals you choose influences your character."

CHAPTER 2 :

PASSIONATE VISION

A CHAMPION LIFE MISSION

For many people life is a chore, or perhaps a struggle to 'make ends meet'. Work is something that 'has' to be done to pay the bills, and fun and leisure are things you do when you're not working. Similarly for many sportspeople, training is a chore, something that 'has' to be done so as to be able to play in the game on the weekend. Is this you? Are you too busy 'earning a living' to design a life of fulfilment and contribution? Are you so focused on winning, that you've forgotten to enjoy the process?

Champion sportspeople, and elite performers in any field, share a different attitude to life, work, and their training. For champions, there is no distinction between work and play, or between training and competition. For champions, their life *is* their work; their daily training *is* their Olympic performance or Wimbledon final.

Champions have learned how to find and live a *life mission*.

IMPORTANCE OF A LIFE MISSION

I think it's important to understand that human beings, contrary to the popular theories of biology, psychology and sociology, are not just a result of genetics or past socialisation processes. We are not just a consequence of our past, but also, and perhaps even more importantly, *a presequence of our future*!

We are not just a consequence of our past, but also,
a presequence of our future!

Rather than a result of our past experiences, I believe human behaviours, feelings, values, attitudes, beliefs and actions are also a consequence of an *impulse to actualise a future self into being*. There is a call within us all, a movement within our self to become something more - without reference to the past.

There is a dream within everyone, a vision or sense of purpose, which through following that dream, enables us to realise our full potential and experience true fulfilment and satisfaction in life.

Champion sportspeople are those who have found that vision within and have found a way to bring it into reality.

Sadly, few people ever have the courage or wherewithal to seek out and live this inner dream - they give up the search for their personal life mission in favour of 'making a living'. Champions in all walks of life are those who have discovered that mission within themselves, and have found, or made, a way to bring it to reality.

40

It could be said that there is no greater goal than for an individual to find a *meaning* for their existence - and in fact, people without a strong sense of purpose or meaning in their life are often unhappy and dissatisfied with their life - regardless of their status, power, possessions or financial wealth.

There is no greater goal than to find a *meaning* for your existence.

If you look in the nearest hospital or mental clinic, the individuals who most frequently suffer from depression, or other chronic physical or mental illnesses, are those who have no meaningful purpose in their life - they have no strong reason to live for and be healthy.

The same importance of a personal meaning for existence was found in the experiences of POWs in concentration camps during World War 2, and in Vietnam. Those prisoners who did not have a strong sense of purpose or mission for their lives, and were not able to see past their current incarceration to a more positive future, lost their will to live, and quickly succumbed to disease, mental illness, or suicide.

In contrast, individuals with a strong sense of personal mission and purpose in their lives are among the greatest achievers and contributors in society. In fact, a characterising trait of any truly successful person is an alignment with their life mission.

Truly successful people have an alignment with their life mission.

WHAT EXACTLY IS A LIFE MISSION?

A life mission could be defined as a 'big picture' for your life. An over-riding purpose that represents everything you are, and believe in. A life mission unifies all your values, attitudes, beliefs and behaviours, and lends a congruency and power to them - because everything you do and say is referenced to that larger vision. There is no internal conflict within you, because you know who you are, what you believe in, and where you're going.

A life mission unifies all your values, attitudes, beliefs and behaviours, and provides congruency and personal power.

This kind of inner congruency and purposeful direction lends you an incredible personal power and emotional momentum, which is in stark contrast to individuals who have internal indecision, lack of direction, and incongruency in their behaviour. A useful analogy is that of a team of dynamic people working together towards a common goal, compared to a group of individuals bickering among themselves and getting nowhere fast. *You* are essentially a team - made up of your body, emotions, beliefs, attitudes, values and actions. When everything you do, feel and think are united in one direction, then you're a 'team' within yourself, and you're able to engage and harness the synergy, or 'team energy', of your whole self working together.

When everything you do, feel and think are united in one direction, you can harness the synergy of your 'whole self'.

DILT'S NEUROLOGICAL LEVELS

The mechanism whereby this unifying synergy of a life mission operates within us can be understood by referring to Robert Dilt's Neurological Levels of human subjective experience. He suggests that there are natural neurological levels, or hierarchies, of our subjective experience; each level 'controlling' the information on the levels below it.

There are six 'neurological levels' of human subjective experience.

These six levels are [# 1 being the highest level] :

 # 1. Mission or Vision
 # 2. Self Identity
 # 3. Values and Beliefs
 # 4. Strategies, Capabilities and States
 # 5. Behaviours
 # 6. External Environment or Context

Each higher level becomes less concrete and general, and yet it has a greater impact on our behaviour and experience. So changing something on a higher level would almost always change things on the lower levels; but changing something on a lower level could, but may not, affect the higher levels.

Hence an individual's mission or vision will affect their sense of self identity, their beliefs and values, the capabilities, strategies and states they employ in their life, the specific behaviours they engage in, and the environments and contexts in which they choose to live and work.

Explaining each of these levels in more detail:

The level of 'External Environment or Context' refers to the specific external conditions in which a behaviour takes place - the where and when, and unique opportunities and constraints in which any behaviour occurs.

The level of 'Behaviours' refers to the automatic and unconscious habits and reactions we engage in, that have little conscious strategy or design; while the level of 'Strategies, Capabilities and States' refers to how we consciously adapt and utilise classes of behaviours to suit broader contexts - how we plan and utilise our resources to achieve outcomes.

The level of 'Values and Beliefs' refers to how we justify or discourage particular strategies or plans - the permissions, reasonings, and whys that motivate or inhibit our behaviours; while the level of 'Self Identity' establishes a sense of self by consolidating sets of beliefs and values into a specific self image, and providing a sense of 'Who I am'.

A life mission provides a sense of direction and purpose for your life.

Finally, as stated earlier, the level of 'Mission or Vision' is defined as a 'big picture' for your life. An over-riding purpose that represents everything you are and believe in, and which unifies all your values, attitudes, beliefs and behaviours, and provides a sense of direction and purpose for your life.

Therefore, changes which affect an individual's sense of 'Mission' or 'Self Identity' have the most widespread and profound effects.

For instance, let's say an individual has a self identity and a purpose in life as a professional sportsperson, then a serious injury makes them unable to continue in that life mission - and let's say they choose to take up study in sports journalism to establish a career in this new field.

The resulting change in their life purpose will affect their sense of self identity;   it may also affect the person's beliefs and attitudes as they face the challenges of becoming a 'student' again;   they will need to learn and develop new capabilities;   they will be doing different things;   and they will probably be working and living in different environments.

> **Your life mission affects your sense of self, your beliefs and values, the capabilities and strategies you use, your specific behaviours, and the environments you choose to live in.**

In contrast, someone may choose to work in a different city, or play for a different sports team (both of which are 'Environment' issues), or may change a 'Behaviour', (such as giving up smoking, or perhaps taking up a new sport), without greatly affecting their beliefs and values, sense of self, or life mission.

It's also important to recognise that having an inner congruency between all these neurological levels provides a strong foundation for success in any endeavour. Conversely, if there is a conflict between any levels, this can create interference and prevent an individual from achieving their potential. For example, someone might have the *capabilities* to be a successful professional athlete, but they may sabotage their chances if they don't have positive *beliefs* and a strong *self identity* that supports those skills.

Likewise, an individual may have a powerful, confident *self image* and strong positive *beliefs* in their ability to be an effective coach or manager, but if they don't develop the interpersonal 'people skills' and the self motivation to succeed, (the *capabilities or strategies* for success), then they will also fail to perform to their potential.

Since the higher levels 'instruct' and influence the lower levels, it can be argued that someone with a strong positive self identity and positive beliefs would probably find a way to develop the necessary capabilities and strategies to succeed - though of course this may not always be the case, and there are many examples of self confident incompetents, (particularly in psychology)!

An individual with a strong life mission and confident self identity will usually develop the positive strategies and capabilities necessary to succeed.

On the other hand, someone with good capabilities, but a poor self image, or lacking a clear sense of life purpose, is unlikely to automatically make the necessary personal changes - and this is readily observable in day to day life, with thousands of people with obvious 'talent' that remains under utilised because of a lack of self confidence, or a strong sense of life mission.

Lets consider a sports example. There are athletes who are able to perform well in a particular situation (*behaviour*); but who don't have a strategy (*capability*), that allows them to succeed in different contexts. Even with good capabilities and skills, some sports people do not believe success or 'winning' is important (*beliefs*), and so don't put in their best efforts, and consequently never achieve their potential in their chosen sport.

Likewise, there are athletes who have the capabilities to perform well and who believe it is important, yet don't always perceive themselves as successful athletes (*identity*). Also there are sports people who seem to have everything going for them - the capabilities, the positive beliefs and self confidence - yet they drift, and never seem to get to the top because they are not in touch with a strong sense of life mission (*mission*); they have no overwhelming sense of purpose in their life.

Sow a thought - harvest an action;
Sow an action - harvest a habit;
Sow a habit - harvest a character;
Sow a character - harvest a fulfilled life.

Another way of understanding the influence of these six neurological levels on our performance is to consider the following statements, which indicate limitations in the speaker's model in the different levels. You can see and understand how simply listening to someone's language can provide an indicator of how they limit, or empower, themselves:

"I don't know what to do with my life."   [*Mission*]
"I'm not a morning person."   [*Identity*]
"I'm always a slow starter."   [*Identity*]
"It takes a long time to get to the top."   [*Belief*]
"The team doesn't travel well."   [*Belief*]
"I don't know how to handle the media."   [*Capability*]
"She has a weak backhand."   [*Capability*]
"I don't know what to do here."   [*Behaviour*]
"How do I do this technique?"   [*Behaviour*]
"The wet weather made playing difficult."   [*Environment*]

FINDING YOUR LIFE MISSION

Given the fact that there are so few people who seem to have, and are living, such a life mission, you'd think it was a very difficult thing - yet identifying and feeling attraction to your life mission is the easiest thing in the world! I choose to believe that *we are all born with a life mission*, and it is our duty to find that precious purpose within us - and to use all our courage, strength and personal gifts to make it a reality.

**Finding your life mission is easy -
Making it a reality is the challenge!**

The challenge comes in sticking to your inner vision, and living your mission in the face of the everyday challenges and obstacles that beset us all. Yet, I believe that if everyone was doing their life mission, there would be less crime, depression, and poverty in the world.

The easiest way to identify your life mission is to simply ask yourself: "What am I really *passionate* about?" "What excites me, and gives me a feeling of deep personal satisfaction?"

**Ask yourself : "What am I really *passionate* about?"
"What really excites me, and gives me a feeling of
deep personal satisfaction?"**

Sometimes, when you're not used to listening within to yourself, the lines of communication are a bit frayed or distorted, so you need to do a few things to find your life mission.

If you're not sure of your life mission, one solution is to use what's known in NLP as the 'as if' frame. Simply ask yourself, "If I *was* sure of my life mission, what would it be?" Then take a guess. Your guess will be informed by that deeper unconscious part of you, that does know.

If you *were* sure of what your life mission was, what would it be?

You can also ask yourself: "Why am I doing what I'm doing?" Are you currently happy and fulfilled doing that job, working in that career?" If not, what would you *rather* be doing? [Answers such as "Lying on the beach", "Holidaying", or "Sleeping" are not allowable responses - it has to be some useful work or career; something where you're making a contribution to society]

Some people never get around to deciding on a life purpose because they don't seem to have any clear direction one way or another. Others are simply afraid of making a 'wrong' decision. They are waiting for ten doves to swoop over their head when they have the right idea, so they know that's the 'right' path!

Another exercise is to imagine being at the end of your life .... what would you like to be able to look back on and say that you had contributed? How is the world, your country, or your local community, a better place because *you* have lived? Take 20 minutes now to do the exercise on 'Finding Your Life Mission'. Find a quiet place, put on some calming relaxation music, and do a short relaxation exercise to settle your body, calm your emotions, and centre your thoughts. [Sample relaxation exercises are provided in Chapter 5 of *Sportsmind*] Do have a pen and paper handy for writing down your thoughts.

EXERCISE : Finding Your Life Mission

1. Imagine your future as a 'timeline' going off in a particular direction. See tomorrow, next month, next year, ten years from now, twenty and thirty years in the future, and further off in the distance, a ripe old age.

2. Now imagine floating up out of your body, and travelling along and above your future timeline to that time in your old age. Notice as you travel, the images and sounds that you sense as you travel the future.

3. Step into your old-age self, and look back over your life, feeling a sense of great satisfaction and accomplishment. See what you did in your time here; listen to your future self tell you about your life mission. Identify the beliefs, values, capabilities, and personal qualities you developed.

4. Return to the present, bringing with you a sense of connection to your life mission.

5. Hold this sense of your life mission and think about how this mission now affects :
  - your self identity; who are you as the holder of this
    life mission?
  - your beliefs and values; what do you need to believe
    and value to achieve this life mission?
  - your capabilities; what capabilities and strategies will
    you develop in order to manifest your life mission?
  - your environment; where will you be, who will you be
    with, and what will you be doing as your life mission?

Spend five to ten minutes writing down your thoughts.

MANIFESTING A VISION

Now that you have identified your life mission, I want to spend a little time in the final section of this chapter talking about how to manifest it - how to bring it into reality. The best way to do this is to provide you with an example, and the best example I can think of is my own process of manifesting my life mission - creating the *Sportsmind* vision.

CASE STUDY : The *Sportsmind* Vision
In 1979 while studying for a degree in Environmental Science, I became dissatisfied with what I perceived as the inconsistencies between the 'ideal' of university education, (ie. the search for knowledge through following a self directed path of study), and the reality of being forced to complete subjects in which I had little interest, and which seemed irrelevant to me.

This sense of frustration led to my withdrawing from study and searching for what I really wanted to do in my life. This search soon led me to the Findhorn Foundation community in Scotland. This community was established in the early 1960's, and since then it has become a 'centre' for an eclectic range of personal growth philosophies and ideals.

My primary reason for travelling to the community at the time, was an interest in their approach to 'organic' agriculture, however during my six month stay I had the opportunity to meet, and attend training workshops with, John Syer and Chris Connolly who had recently developed their *Sporting Body, Sporting Mind* approach to the psychological training of sportspeople. This experience - both my stay in the community and the work with John and Chris - was a major influence upon me and the beliefs I held, and resulted in a significant shift in both my sense of personal identity and sense of purpose for my life.

Two of the core principles of both the Findhorn community and *Sporting Body, Sporting Mind*, are the belief in a greater human potential that is reached through developing awareness; and that more can be achieved, and in a more fulfilling way, through co-operative effort than through competitive individuality. This was demonstrated in practice, daily, in work in the community, and demonstrated in the *Sporting Body, Sporting Mind* training through the sport of volleyball, of which John Syer was both an ex-national level player and coach.

For the first time in my life I was absolutely inspired by two people who I admired, and aspired to be like - and at that moment I knew I wanted to do something similar in Australia. I had found my life mission: to facilitate *Sportsmind* training programs which would be a vehicle for both enhancing sports performance, and of personal development.

When I returned to Australia in the Autumn of 1980, I went back to complete my degree, (changing my main studies program from Agriculture / Ecology to Social Psychology), while continuing my own personal search in the areas of personal growth psychology, (attending many workshops and courses, and quickly discovering Neuro-Linguistic Programming).

Later in that same year I designed and attempted to market the first *Sportsmind* training workshops in which the concept of playing sport was seen as a vehicle of self actualisation and personal development. These first programs were abject failures!

I think I had four people in the first workshop, and only one person interested in the second which I promptly cancelled! I then decided to give up on the idea of *Sportsmind*, and went back to complete my degree in Environmental Management, studying part time and supporting myself with work as a kitchen hand.

While I excelled in my studies, I found little passion for them, and no sense of satisfaction, and I chose to study a wide range of subjects in my final year - including Japanese language, during which time I came across the concepts of Accelerated Learning, which I applied in my studies, and ended up topping the class!

This led to my conducting some informal 'lessons' on Accelerated Learning and NLP for other students at the university - who likewise improved their academic performances significantly. These classes were foundational in my recognising that the only time I felt really inspired was when I was *teaching a personal development program.* I had again found my life purpose.

However, after word spread of the success of my study classes, the university hierarchy chose to stop them, (despite their obvious success) - since I did not have a 'qualification' in teaching. However by that time I had managed to convince a number of TAFE colleges to allow me to teach programs for them, which were again very successful, and I decided to become a 'legitimate' teacher by obtaining a teaching diploma.

I had obtained my Practitioner and Master Practitioner certificates in NLP by 1986, so when I began my teaching studies in 1990, I was appalled to find that there was nothing in the curriculum about either NLP and sensory preference in learning, nor was there any information about any of the Accelerated Learning techniques which I had been teaching informally for years! I quickly recognised that I knew more about teaching than the lecturers, and that much of what was being taught to teachers was out-of-date, and even counter-productive to successful learning!

After excelling in my first semester, at the beginning of second semester we were introduced to the current system of school 'assessment' practices which we were expected to adhere to.

These assessment practices were based on *comparative assessment* - ie. comparing one student to another, for no better purpose than to determine who is 'better' than someone else, and therefore who should go to university, (regardless of the fact that studies have clearly shown that success at university bears little relationship to school results). Further, it has been clearly demonstrated time and again that *learning is far more successful for the majority of students in an environment of co-operative learning,* and that comparative assessment is extremely counter productive to both learning and self esteem. Despite these facts, we were expected to toe the line.

I refused to further degrade students' learning and self esteem with such archaic practices, and so withdrew from the course.

I had heard about an innovative school at the University of Western Sydney that offered research degrees in areas of one's own choosing - finally a university which allowed students to follow their own learning path! - and so I decided to re-visit the *Sportsmind* concept, and designed a research project to investigate the uses of NLP in sports performance enhancement.

So began my five year M.Sc.(Hons) thesis which resulted in the *Sportsmind* book, six performance enhancement audio tapes, 96 *Sportsmind* workshops conducted from Cairns to Warnambool with 1,247 attendants, and 214 radio, newspaper and television interviews as part of an education campaign in Psychological Skills Training for the Australian sporting community.

The interesting thing to me, given the magnitude and outstanding results of my research project, (which is unequalled anywhere in the world in sport psychology research), was the general apathy of the existing sporting organisations, such as the AIS and state sporting academies, towards my work.

Again, it was a case of not quite belonging to the coterie of 'proper' academics, because I used NLP in my work! Even at the writing of this work, and despite the thousands of testimonials about *Sportsmind* I've received from athletes and coaches, the majority of sport psychologists still refuse to acknowledge either NLP, or the work I've done in the sports applications of NLP.

Since the completion of my Masters degree in 1997, I have furthered my ultimate vision for *Sportsmind* by designing a twelve module correspondence course, and a *Sportsmind - NLP Practitioner* certification course, with the aim of educating a network of very capable *Sportsmind* performance consultants who will be able to positively enhance the performance of sportspeople of all ages, ability levels and sports interest.

The reason for sharing this rather long and drawn out story with you is to encourage you to recognise that even when you have identified your life mission, be prepared to stand up for what you know in your heart is right. Refuse to compromise your values and beliefs in the face of social mores or current academic views.

Recognise that the process of manifesting your life mission will require the development of specific *personal qualities* in you. Qualities such as *persistence*; *self belief*; *courage* (particularly in the face of criticism or when attempting something untried); *self confidence* (even in the face of setbacks or even outright failures); *positive motivation* (which of course comes out of clarity in goal setting and planning), and of course *organisational skills*, to name a few.

Over the next chapters I will be going into more detail about *how* to manifest your life mission by developing within yourself these positive qualities - these champion thoughts and feelings.

"You are a champion because you never give up — understanding that true ability comes only through persistence."

CHAPTER 3 :

IRRESISTIBLE MOMENTUM

BUILDING CHAMPION MOMENTUM

The key to your being successful in sport, or any endeavour, will not be as a result of a different diet, or through a new cross training regimen, or with the latest technologically advanced running shoes, or the latest software package, or gee-whiz laptop computer - it will be a result of your ability to establish and maintain *physical, emotional and mental momentum* toward the realisation of your life mission.

Understanding, and employing, the principles of *making things happen* allows you to turn that life mission from an attractive dream into a fulfilling reality by chunking it down into achievable goals and action plans.

Champions understand how to generate *irresistible personal momentum* to turn their *dreams into reality*.

TURNING DREAMS INTO REALITY

Once you have identified a life mission for your self - a personal vision which you have committed yourself to - the next step is to go about achieving it! Having a dream is important - but lots of people have dreams, yet they never achieve them. So how *do* you turn dreams into reality?

> **Having a positive vision is important, but you also want to have a *strategy* to achieve it.**

One of the keys is to understand how you got to be where you are now - because where you are, now, was at one time just a dream wasn't it? There was a time, for instance, when you hadn't even started playing or competing in your chosen sport, or working in your current career - and to reach the level or position you're currently at now was just a dream. Isn't it so?

So what was it that brought *that dream* into reality? What is it that precedes all your actions, all of your behaviours, and all of your performances in every area of your life? It's your *decisions*.

> **Your decisions determine *who* you become.**

Your decisions precede all your actions and therefore *determine who you become*. Everything in you life, including your current sports performances and your current level of financial and career success, is determined by the decisions you have made, and are making right now. Your decisions determine what you think, how you feel, what you do, and who you become.

THE POWER OF DECISIONS

If you're wondering why someone is currently achieving a greater level of success than you - in any area - then the answer is simply that they have made different decisions than you.

Different decisions about how they spend their time; different decisions about how they respond to setbacks or 'defeats'; different decisions about who they hang around with; different decisions about their approach to training or work. But most importantly, different decisions about what they expect of themselves, and about what they *want* to achieve in their sport, career, and personal life.

> **Differences in people reflect the different decisions they have made.**

Yet, unfortunately, most people don't make these kinds of decisions consciously - they just *hope* they do well, and then *wish* they had done better! However, hopes and wishes are not good enough for champions - nor are they good enough for *you*!

Recognise that if you *don't* consciously make these kinds of decisions - about what level of performance you expect of yourself, and what you want in your life - then you've really made a decision by default anyway. You've decided to let *other people*, or the whims of the environment, direct your destiny.

> **If *you* don't decide what you want, then your destiny is in the hands of *other people*.**

No one likes to think they're being controlled by other people, yet I hear time and again *excuses* why people haven't achieved more in their career, in their sport, or financially. "I don't have the right build"; "I'm too old"; "I haven't had the opportunity"; "I haven't got the experience"; "I don't have enough time"; and so on.

I'm sure you've heard similar excuses, and perhaps you've used some of them yourself - I know I used to, and I still occasionally fall into this trap. Yet I quickly realise, as I hope you do, that as Anthony Robbins says, all these things are *conditions - and it's not the conditions in your life that hold you back, but rather your decisions!*

It's not the *conditions* in your life that hold you back, but rather your *decisions*!

What you *decide* to do, given whatever conditions you currently have in your life, makes the difference in your performances.

Of course you can argue that some people are born with certain advantages - a fantastic sports physique, financial resources, a supportive family, or an opportune environment. However, lots of those people, even given these advantages don't achieve their potential, do they? They're not as successful as they could be.

Then there are other people, coming from the poorest conditions and with physical, environmental and social limitations who shuck off the bonds of those conditions to achieve sporting, political, financial or career performances way beyond expectations.

How do they do it? Simply by making committed decisions. The power of a committed decision cannot be underestimated.

TRUE DECISIONS

However, for your decisions to make a real difference in your life, they have to be *true* decisions. Many people don't understand what a true decision is - they use the word loosely, and so decisions for them have become just *preferences*, things they'd *like* to have happen, rather than real decisions.

The power of a *committed decision* cannot be underestimated.

In contrast, a true decision evokes a firm commitment to make it happen, leaving no choice for any other option. For instance, if you make such a committed decision to give up smoking, then that's it, you'll do it, and you no longer even consider the possibility of your smoking again. If you truly decide to reduce your golf handicap by five strokes over the next six months, then that's it - you'll do it. If you truly decide to improve your fitness, or lose weight, or increase your monthly income, then you'll make it happen.

However, most people state preferences rather than make committed decisions: "I'd like to give up smoking"; "I'd like to improve my percentage of first services in court"; "I hope I get the promotion"; "I hope I'm selected for the team"; or "I'd like to earn more money this year" - all of which are just wish lists, and have no power to positively change your life or performances.

Preferences and wishes have no power to positively change your life or performance.

MAKING YOUR GOALS _DECISIONS_

Here's a little exercise for you to do. Think right now about a true decision you've made recently - something you definitely decided on, and followed through with. A decision about buying a new car, or house, taking up a new job, or maybe even the decision to buy this book! Notice _how_ you thought about it, and identify the exact moment when you actually _decided_ - when you said "Yes, I'll do it".

Now think about something you've been 'considering', but haven't made a definite decision about yet. Again notice _how_ you think about that, and compare the differences in what you see, hear, and feel to the time you made a definite decision. You'll notice that you think about the two experiences very differently.

People think about definite decisions very differently from issues yet undecided.

Now consider: _how_ have you been thinking about your life mission, and the dreams you've identified for yourself? Is it more similar to the first way, or to the second? _Are you thinking about your life mission like a true decision, or just something you're 'considering', that you'd like to achieve but haven't really committed yourself to yet?_ You want to think about achieving your dreams in the same way that you think about getting a loaf of bread from the shop - simple, easy, no questions - I'll just do it.

Think about getting your dreams in the same way as getting a loaf of bread from the shop.

COMMITMENT TO ACTION

So you want to think about your dreams as true decisions, not just preferences - but how do I know if I've made a committed decision? *True decisions are always followed by actions.*

For instance, if you truly decide to buy a new car, you'll go and see a car dealer, or place an add in the paper to sell your old one. If you truly decide to end a relationship, you'll confront your partner and talk about it, or you'll pack your bags! And if you make a true decision to play to a higher standard in your sport, or reach a cherished sports goal, *then you'll do something about it - you'll take some action.* Until the point of action, it's just been something you've been 'considering' - *action* makes it a decision.

True decisions are always followed by action.

The interesting thing is that when you make a definite commitment to a particular decision, it unlocks the energy within you to achieve it. I'm sure you've had the experience of agonising over a decision about something for days or perhaps even weeks - you know how such indecision can totally sap your drive, because you have no clear direction. However, as soon as you've hopped off the fence and decided one way or the other, you're able to start moving again. In the next moment, right now, you could use the power of a true decision to change your life. The motivation, the power, the energy to succeed comes from making committed decisions.

Motivation comes from making decisions.

TWO IMPORTANT DECISIONS

Two decisions I made that really changed my life, were the decision eight years ago to get rid of the television set, and the decision to avoid negative, pessimistic people. It's amazing how much you can achieve when you don't own a TV! I've been much more successful in achieving my career, financial, sporting, and family goals since I removed it. Of course I still enjoy watching TV when I go on holiday, (it's a bit of a novelty then), but I would never have it in my personal living space ever again. So give away your television set, and use the extra time you will now have to advance you goals!

If you want to be more successful, try throwing away the television set!

Secondly, my time is too important to me to spend it around negative, complaining people. You can earn more money, you can get a new job, you can find a new relationship - but you only have a limited time here, and you can't beg, borrow or steal one second more. So why waste your time putting up with people who you don't like being around, and who drag you down? Blood may be thicker than water, but this doesn't mean you have to spend time with relatives if they're negative and pessimistic!

Anyway, I believe *your true family is that collection of people who share your similar high aspirations, beliefs and values*, and who are positive and encouraging of your goals - not necessarily those you're genetically related to. Negative people can drain your energy levels, your enthusiasm, and your confidence. Choose to spend time around positive people who, like you, are committed to reaching high goals, and fulfilling a positive life mission.

YOUR FOCUS OF ATTENTION

There is one particular decision that you're making all the time that's especially important - that is, *your decision about what to focus your attention on.* At each moment, what you decide to pay attention to, and what you decide to focus your thinking on, affects how you feel, and what you do.

What you decide to focus your thinking on affects how you feel, and what you do.

For example, consider a game of golf. You tee up your ball on the first hole, (a par 5), and hit a glorious drive straight down the middle of the fairway - the best drive you've done for ages! Feeling good, you walk down to the ball and take out your 3 wood, again striking the ball sweetly and watch with pleasure as it comes to rest just an easy pitch from the green! You walk up confidently, take out your wedge, and with a smooth flowing swing, connect solidly with the ball, and watch in bliss as it sails in a perfect arc directly for the pin.

Suddenly, a freak gust of wind drifts your ball into the steep right hand bunker!

Now, what you decide to focus your attention on at that moment determines how you feel and how you perform! What do many people choose to focus on in such an instance? The misfortune of going into the bunker, perhaps thinking things like: "There goes my birdie chance now"; or "I hate *that* bunker; I never play it well. Last time I was in *that* bunker, it took me three shots to get out, and I ended up with a triple bogey"; or "I always manage to mess up a good drive"; or even "There goes my round today".

In order to do better at something, it's useful to ask the question, "What do the top people focus on at any point in time, and in particular circumstances?". In this instance, invariably champion golfers focus on their strongly desired goal, and committed standard of performance. They choose to focus their attention on the excellent drives they just did, and on previous good bunker shots, and imagine successfully getting up and down in two, to still make birdie, rather than on the fact of landing in the bunker.

Champions focus on their strongly desired goal, and committed standard of performance.

I like to suggest that we human beings are a lot like guided missiles - we move toward whatever we regularly and consistently focus on and picture in our imagination and thoughts, with feeling. It's not what you think about occasionally that's important, but what you're consistently and regularly focusing your attention upon that influences your life, and performance.

Think for a minute about when you were a child - didn't you imagine yourself playing a particular sport as you watched your heroes play, and think to yourself, "I'm going to do that!" Likewise, we first *imagine ourselves* into every new job, relationship, activity and performance, before we do it in reality.

We first *imagine ourselves* into every new job, relationship, activity and performance.

So realise that *your decisions about what you focus your attention upon are directing your life.*

Ask your self, right now, "What have I been thinking about most this week? What has my focus been upon? What have I spent most of my time thinking about?"

I think it's interesting to note that for many people, their focus is often on what *other* people are doing : the latest office gossip; which celebrities have been sleeping with whom; the racing form or details of the recent performances of their favourite sports star. Champions tend to be much more concerned with *themselves* and their life to focus for too long on other people.

Champions tend to be focused on themselves, and their performance.

Every thought has one of only two consequences - it either moves you closer to your dreams, or it takes you further away. There are no other choices, or 'idle' thoughts! What you decide to think about moves you in that direction.

Every thought either moves you closer to your dreams, or takes you further away.

However, many people allow their focus to be distracted by other people and events, rather than being directed by their own dreams and desires. For many people, life is like a river, and they're just floating along with the current - current fashions and fads, current events and current problems. The trouble is that sometimes that current can smash you into the rocks or over the waterfall - so it's a good idea to have a direction in mind for where you want to go, and regularly and consistently focus your thinking on that.

CHUNKING DOWN YOUR DREAMS

There are thousands of people with 'dreams' - but only a handful ever make them into reality. How do they do it? Simply, by just:
1. **Committing to their dream - by** *deciding* **to do it;**
2. **Regularly and consistently** *imagining* **achieving it;**
3. **Turning the dream into specific, focused** *goals*; **and**
4. **Establishing a step-wise** *action plan* **to make it happen.**

In the last chapter, and the previous sections in this chapter, I've covered in detail how to identify and commit yourself to a dream, or a life mission, and the importance of positively visualising yourself successfully attaining it. However an essential skill in realising any life mission is the ability to 'chunk down' your 'big picture' into 'bite-sized' pieces. To be able to break the dream down into specific, focused *goals and action plans*.

> **An essential skill in realising a life mission is to 'chunk it down' into 'bite-sized' pieces.**

The only thing that will keep you going when the going gets tough - that will get you up early and working late at night - is a dream, focused into a set of specific goals and action plans.

The only thing that will keep you fighting to win when it's five games to one and match point against you, and it's hot and you're tired, is a dream. The only thing that will keep you out there in the cold and rain at training, when you're soaking wet and uncomfortable, is a dream. The only thing that will get you up and pushing forward to make another tackle in the last minutes of the game when you're body is bruised and exhausted, is a dream. Nothing else will.

WHY DON'T PEOPLE SET GOALS?

Recently, I was invited to give a *Sportsmind* presentation to a group of aspiring young athletes who had just been selected as the best in their sport in their region, and were being inducted into an elite sports training academy. One of the first questions I asked them was how many of them had written down goals. The answer ..... five out of sixty! And these kids were supposedly the great sporting hopes for the region!

Why don't people set goals?

I then asked the question: "Well, why don't people set goals?" They answered with the four most common reasons:
1. The 'couldn't be bothered' response; the deadly apathetic malaise.
2. The 'don't want to appear different from peers' response - a typically Australian disease.
3. The fear of failure - if I don't set a goal, then I can't fail at getting it.
4. The fear of success - how responsible/guilty/afraid I'd feel if I was incredibly successful.

There are four reasons why people don't set goals: apathy; fear of being different; fear of failure; and fear of success.

I wonder if I asked <u>you</u> to show me <u>your</u> written down goals for the next six months, twelve months, and three to five years ...... would you have anything to show me?

If not, why not? Are any of the responses above applicable to you in your sport, career, and life?

You know, a lot of athletes train very hard in the belief that it's hard training that leads inevitably to success. They read about how their idols train; they copy their gym routines and dietary habits; they do everything *physically* that they do, believing that if they train hard and do all the things that the top performers do - then they'll also succeed. *But it doesn't work that way!*

Th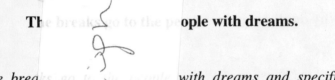**ople with dreams.**

*The brea*ks go fo the people *with dreams and specific goals.* You wan to have a dream goal. Somehow, the dream itself provides the motivation nd the means for its own accompl shment.

If you're interested, I've included a lot of practical ideas on goal achieving in Chapter 2 of *Sportsmind*, and I want to remind you to consider this: *there is power in knowing what you want*, and in committing yourself to achieve it, and this is especially true in sport. Champions in every area of life are consistent goal setters and planners. Realise that in six months, you're going to become *some* one. In a year, you'll be doing *some* thing. In five years, you're going to be playing at *some* standard in your sport. In ten years, you're going to be earning *some* level of income.

Decide, right now, who you're going to be, what you're going to be doing, and what you're going to have in the future.

Why leave these things to chance, or to the whims of the environment, or someone else's plans? Why not decide - right now - who you're going to be, what you're going to be doing, and what you're going to have - in twelve months, five years, and ten years from now?

Here's a quick little exercise. On a sheet of paper, quickly write down *the three most important goals* you want to achieve in six months, twelve months, and within three to five years - all of which will be part of bringing about your larger purpose. Having done the life mission exercise from the previous chapter, this should be easy. Take fifteen minutes to do this now.

An important point to remember is that most people *over-estimate* what they can practically achieve in a year, yet greatly *under-estimate* what they can achieve in ten years, or over their lifetime.

> **Most people *over-estimate* what they can do in a year, yet *under-estimate* what they can achieve in ten years, or over their lifetime.**

Also, you want to set yourself goals that are almost out of reach; goals that require great physical, emotional and mental efforts to achieve. Remember that if you aim for mediocre goals, that's likely what you'll achieve. If you aim for greatness, you may well reach it. But you'll never know your true potential and untapped talents until you really test yourself.

> **Aim for mediocrity, and that's what you'll get.**
> **Aim for greatness, and you may well reach it.**

S.M.A.R.T.E.R. GOALS

I think it's important to note that just writing down your goals is not enough, because some people will have a dream, chunk it down into specific goals, and even write them down - and yet still not achieve them. The reason this happens is that they didn't know *how* to set, and work with, their goals properly. For your goals to be effective they will want to adhere to the following seven S.M.A.R.T.E.R. goal achieving principles. If your goals adhere to these simple principles, *you will definitely achieve them*. If they don't, chances are you won't get there.

S = **Specific and measurable**
M = **'Me' focused - controllable by myself**
A = **Achievable**
R = **Reviewed regularly**
T = **Timed**
E = **Ecological - consider 'whole' self**
R = **Reasons and Reward**

Some people don't set goals at all; others set them, but don't write them down; still others write them down, but don't know how to work with them effectively. These S.M.A.R.T.E.R. goal setting principles provide an easy and practical method of defining precisely what you want, a checking system to make sure your goals are achievable and in line with your current beliefs and values, and a mechanism for ensuring you follow through with them. I want to now look at, and explain, how each of the seven principles works to help you achieve your goals.

As we go through them, check the goals you've written to ensure they meet the criteria - if they don't, then alter them so they do.

S = Specific and measurable

Ensure your goals are specific and measurable. What *precisely* do you want? Rather than writing "I want to get better at tennis", or "I want to lose weight", or "I want to play well in the game this weekend", identify the *specific level* you want to attain. Some examples might be: "To be a trim and toned 75kg"; "To reduce my golf handicap by 3 strokes"; "To achieve 70% of my first services in court"; "To earn $80,000 this financial year".

M = 'Me' focused - controllable by myself

Your goals want to be *controllable by yourself*. Goals such as "I want to marry X", or "I want my son to be a concert pianist", or even "I'm going to win the golf tournament", are not under your control. X might not want to marry you, your son may not want to become a concert pianist, and winning is a result of how well you play, and how well your opponents play, on the day.

More controllable goals would be: "I'm going to ask X out on a date" (you can control *your asking* - not their going); or "I'm going to provide my son with the opportunities and encouragement to become a concert pianist"; or "I'm going to hit 80 or better today", (which if everyone else plays about to their handicap, will see me win the tournament).

You can't control winning, you *can* control your effort, your concentration, enthusiasm, and your attitude.

It's important to recognise that you can't control winning - but you *can* control your level of effort, your enthusiasm, your concentration, and your attitude. So some people suggest that rather than focusing on the *outcome*, (winning), you direct all your attention to the *process*, (the *means* by which you will win).

While I agree on the importance of paying attention to the process, I do think it's also important to still want to win, and to aim to win. I think both are equally important, because athletes, managers, or salespeople who just focus on the 'process' alone in their goal setting, lose the necessary *hunger*, the edge that makes a champion performer. This edge comes from the *desire to win*.

> **People who just focus on the 'process' alone lose the *hunger* that makes a champion.**

So you *want* to win, yet you also want to focus on the *means* by which you will win - the specific skills and techniques that you employ to hit straight down the fairway, or settle a new contract, successfully resolve a negotiation, coach a team, or whatever. This may sound like a paradox, so work with it like this:

EXERCISE : Outcome & Process Goals

1. Picture a series of colour slides, one behind the other. The slide right at the back is the largest, and on it is a picture of your successful *outcome* - winning the tournament, receiving the gold medal, getting the new job, going out with that special person. Associated with this slide is all the good feelings you will have when you successfully achieve it.

2. In front of this big picture, place a series of other slides that represent the steps you will go through to achieve the big picture, and the specific skills you use. Your smooth swing and focused concentration; your excellent communication skills; your positive attitude and powerful self motivation. The *means* by which you will successfully reach your goal.

74

A = Achievable

A is for *achievable*. Make your goals achievable from where you are now. For instance, if you're currently playing B grade tennis, it's not very realistic to set a goal to win the U.S. Open *this* year - you'd just be setting yourself up for a failure. However, if you're a hot young teenage tennis player with a lot of motivation and the desire to reach the top, then setting such a goal for say six or seven years time, might very well be achievable - provided you're willing to put in the effort.

Assess your current abilities and set a goal enough beyond yourself to challenge you and make you want to work toward it, but not something way beyond your current ability, or too easy, or you'll just get discouraged, or bored. Recognise here that your life mission is a really large, grand vision or purpose - which you then chunk down into achievable goals, which you progressively accomplish to advance this grand mission.

If you can't 'see' yourself achieving a goal, then you probably won't.

As a general rule if you can't 'see' yourself achieving a goal, then you probably won't, so aim for something a bit smaller, then when you reach that, shoot for the bigger one.

For example, when I first took up Aikido, I couldn't honestly see myself with a black belt - because the standard of competence and control was so beyond my beginner's abilities - so I set my goal for a brown belt, which I *could* see myself achieving. However, since attaining my brown belt, I *can* now see myself successfully grading to black belt - which is one of my goals to achieve by the end of this year.

R = Reviewed regularly

It's important to remember to regularly review your goals. Build a *positive expectation of success* by regularly thinking about your goals, and imagining what it will be like to achieve them.

Look at your list of written goals at least once every day. Preferably, spend five minutes first thing in the morning, and last thing at night to briefly think about them. This both sets the tone for your whole day by giving you a strong sense of direction right from the moment you wake up, and allows your unconscious resources to provide you with inspiration and ideas as you sleep.

> **Spend five minutes morning and night looking at and imagining your goals.**

I also recommend writing your goals on small palm cards, (about the size of a business card), and carrying them with you throughout the day. Then if you get stuck in traffic, or in a queue at the bank, rather than feeling angry and frustrated, you can use the time productively to think about and imagine achieving them!

Remember, there are no 'idle' thoughts - every thought is an opportunity to plant the seed of a step along the way to achieving what you want in your life. Cultivate a *constructive obsession* about your goals; think about them constantly; dream about them; *want* them.

> **Champions cultivate a *constructive obsession* about their goals.**

CASE STUDY : Michael Atherton and F.E.C.

The best example of the power of regularly reviewing your goals, and creating a constructive obsession like this, is that of Michael Atherton, current captain of the English Cricket team. In his early days playing club and county cricket he got the nickname "F.E.C.", because these initials were written all over his bags and cricket gear - but no one knew what they stood for. Until he a was selected for the English cricket team and appointed captain - of course, they stood for "Future English Captain"!

Now the best part, is that I told that story to a group of aspiring young rowers at St. Joseph's College who were preparing for their yearly regatta against the other schools. One of the boys was wanting to obtain the position of coxswain in the first eight crew. He was currently second in line - the incumbent from last year was performing well, and there was no reason to change him, so this boy not only had to do as well, but better!

When he saw F.E.C., he read it as "First Eight Cox"!

So this lad, when he saw F.E.C., read it as "First Eight Cox"! He then wrote F.E.C. all over his school bags and books; he put up posters of F.E.C. everywhere in his room and on the ceiling above his bed; he put them in the toilet and on the fridge. He drove his parents nuts with his F.E.C. posters everywhere!

Of course, what do you think this lad was thinking about when he went to sleep at night, or when he went to the fridge, or when he took his books out of his bag?

He had created a *constructive obsession* about achieving his goal.

I initially spoke to the boys in November, and gave them two further *Sportsmind* workshops in January and February. At the February workshop the lad's father came up to me to thank me for helping his son attain the first eight coxswain position - which he had been given just the week before. He had reached his goal in just under three months!

What's more, he not only coxed the first eight of the school, but also led them to a resounding victory over their more fancied rivals in the annual 'Head of the River' race just a month later!

Another story is that of the 100m runner Leroy Burrell who, after winning this event at the world championships, and breaking the world record at the time, took out a slip of paper from inside his running shoes and admitted to running that time a thousand times in his mind before the day of the race! He also had cultivated his constructive obsession, and had kept his attention focused on his desired goal by the simple act of keeping a reminder in his shoe!

> **He had run the race *a thousand times in his mind* before the day of the race.**

So *you* can do this too! Whatever it is that you're aiming for, write it on a sheet of paper - make up a colourful poster, and even include photos and drawings if you want - and put it on the ceiling above your bed, or on the back of the toilet door, or on the fridge door, or on your briefcase, or in your wallet, or in *all* these places. The more you start thinking of yourself as *already having the goal, or already the way you want to be*, the faster you will make it happen.

As for me, I'm a C.E.A. - ie., a "Consultant to Elite Athletes"!

Another reason for regularly reviewing your goals is so that you can change and update them as necessary. Many times I've set goals for myself and started working towards them, only to find after six or twelve months, that I needed to change them a bit to adapt them to my new circumstances.

So be flexible with your goals. A daily review of your goals allows this process to happen smoothly and naturally.

It's important to be flexible with your goals.

T = Timed

T stands for setting a specific *time* or target date by which you will achieve the goal. If you don't do this it's too easy to just keep putting it off to 'one day'. Goals have been called 'dreams with a deadline', so set a timeline for your achieving each of your goals.

Goals are dreams with a deadline.

Of course, allow a realistic amount of time for their achievement. Some people fail at goal achieving simply because they either don't set a date for their goals, or they set unrealistic dates and get discouraged when they don't achieve them in the time allowed.

Some examples of specific, timed goals might be: "To swim an Olympic qualifying time in the 100m freestyle at the national titles next month"; "To buy a new house by the end of the year"; "To be selected to play left wing for the first grade side within three years"; "To be financially independent by age 55"; or "To win a major golf tournament within the next five years", and so on.

E = Ecological - consider your 'whole' self

Personal ecology is a concept that recognises that you are a complex organism, made up of different 'parts'. If these parts of yourself get into conflict, then you're not going to function optimally. Ecology means being responsible to your *whole self*, when you set and work toward your goals.

Be responsible to your *whole self* in your goal setting.

This means consider the *other* things that are important in your life, or that you have responsibility for. For example, relationships, work, family, and relaxation. Denying a part of yourself to achieve a goal will only lead to self sabotage, as the part of you that is denied manifests periods of lethargy or unmotivation; excessive nervousness in important competitions; lapses in concentration at crucial moments, or recurrent injuries.

This is one reason why some people don't achieve a particular goal - there is a part of them that doesn't *really* want it to happen, and so it sabotages their performance. Relationships are a common reason for this type of inner sabotage.

For instance, you might set yourself a goal to represent your country in your sport, then as you put more and more time into training, and are away from home more and more frequently, that part of you that needs and values the emotional support of a relationship feels denied, and 'out of the blue' you suddenly get sick, or injure yourself, just before an important selection trial, and miss out on selection. Or after playing really well all season, you have a form slump and put in a pathetic performance - just when the selectors are watching!

This type of thing happens so often in sport, it's no accident! It's a result of *pushing* yourself, rather than working *with* yourself in achieving goals.

If your goals are not compatible with all the other parts of yourself, you may experience self sabotage in some form.

This is why it's so important when setting your goals to really listen to yourself - to pay attention to your feelings. A simple way to do this is to imagine you've actually achieved what you want, and then ask yourself how has your life changed? Does any part of you object to these changes? Then pay attention to any messages that you get - either in the form of images, words or sounds, and especially in your feelings - in response to those questions. Why not try this now?

EXERCISE : Checking for Objections to Goals

1. Pick any goal that you've set yourself to achieve, and take a few minutes to imagine having it, doing it, or being that way. Step into the picture and *feel* what it will be like.

2. Now ask yourself, "How has my life changed?" Think about *all* the different areas of your life: your relationships; your family life; your friends; your work; your income; what you do with your time; how much leisure time you have and how you spend it; and so on.

3. Ask, "Does any part of me object to these changes?" Then listen for any answers or responses that you get.

Interpreting any such answers can occasionally be a bit challenging, particularly if you're not willing to listen objectively, but generally you will know if there's an objection or not. It just won't feel quite right, or you won't be able to see things clearly, or you'll simply get an answer that says, "No!"

If you do get an objection, you will want to negotiate with that part of you before you start working toward the goal. For instance, you might have a part of you objecting to the increased media attention you will get as a result of achieving a major sports goal; or a part of you might feel you can't be a 'nice' person any more once you take on a promotion to a management position at work; or a part of you may object to losing the friendships of current team or work mates, in order to advance your professional career with a move to a different club or job.

> **Unless you resolve any objections, you won't feel fully aligned to your goal.**

So in these instances you will want to find a way to reassure those parts of you that object, and get them on side. Objections can be about anything, and they may even appear insignificant, or silly - but unless they are resolved you won't feel fully aligned to your goal.

In NLP there is a specific process called 'reframing objections' that is particularly useful for dealing with, and resolving such inner conflicts and objections.

> **When you have all of you working together towards a goal, you unlock a store of personal power.**

Try the following exercise if you have conflict about anything - it can also be used for resolving interpersonal conflicts within a team or organisation.

EXERCISE : Reframing Objections

1. Establish communication with the part of you, or the individual in the organisation, that objects to the goal or decision.

2. Identify the *positive intention* behind the objection. What is the positive purpose for the objection? Ask. "What are you trying to do for me, or for the organisation?" [Note: this answer must be a *positive* and useful intention. Answers such as "Trying to make you fail", or "Stopping you from succeeding", or the like are not allowable. If you get such a response, continue by asking "What is the *positive intention* behind *that*?", until you do get to a proper positive response]

3. Ask the part, or individual, if it's possible to come up with at least three other ways of achieving their desired positive intention, and still allow you or the organisation to go for the goal, or make the decision. Is there any *other way* of satisfying their positive intention?

4. If so, have the part or individual come up with at least three other ways of doing so - and commit to doing or using one of these three ways from now on.

5. If not, ask yourself or the other individuals in the organisation, if there is a way to adapt or change the goal to allow it to reflect the concerns of the objecting part or party. Negotiate until a consensus is reached.

CASE STUDIES : Squash, Tennis, Golf and Triathlon

I have used the above six step process of reframing objecting parts very successfully with many sportspeople to help them achieve an inner congruency and 'whole' self alignment to their desired goals and changes in behaviour.

The first example was a squash player who had an inner conflict about whether or not to play in a higher grade - something he wanted, but which a part of him objected to since he had made some wonderful friends in his current team.

The second case was a tennis player who was having an inner conflict between her sport and personal life. Part of her wanted to continue going for her goal of making a successful career out of professional tennis which she had not yet achieved, while another part of her was concerned that she was getting older, and had no current romantic relationship, and her devotion to tennis was preventing her from finding a suitable partner.

The third case was a golfer who had a part of him which was over meticulous and picky, criticising him all the time, and this was sapping his confidence. Through the reframing process, we were able to identify the positive intention behind the behaviour, and develop other ways to achieve this positive intention, which stopped the negative internal dialogue plaguing his game, allowing him to regain confidence in his play.

The final example was a Triathlete who was similarly plagued by a negative, very critical part which was involved in continually negatively comparing his performance with others. Even though he was continually improving his times, this part continued to focus on comparative performance, and this demolished his self esteem. Again we were able to redirect this part's input to more positive avenues of expression.

As you can see, the concept of personal ecology is an important one, and I've chosen to spend a lot of time explaining it in detail. An important point I want to make is that there is nothing so sad as a lonely workaholic - be it in sport or business - deluding themselves that they are successful because they spend all their time training or at work.

It's been said that *if you get to the top of the mountain alone, you'll probably jump off.* Truly successful people in sport and business learn to work with themselves, rather than push and deny themselves, and live a holistic life that makes their eventual success that much sweeter because it is shared with friends, colleagues, and family.

Champions also find a way to contribute to the wider community, through service organisations, or creating their own way of giving back to the Earth and society.

Champions find a way to contribute to the community.

Finally, E also stands for *empower yourself* by giving yourself *permission* to achieve your goals, and know that you're worthy of them. Sometimes, on the verge of success, people sabotage their performance because their self concept is not large enough to accept success. Enlarge your self concept by continually affirming to yourself that you *are* worthy of success and high achievement - you are worthy of being called a champion in your chosen sport, or career.

Give yourself *permission* to achieve your goals, and know that you're worthy of them.

R = Reasons and Reward

The final key in the SMARTER process of goal achieving is to have powerful *reasons* for achieving a goal, and to *reward yourself when you achieve a goal*, or a significant milestone along the way to a goal.

It's a very useful exercise to consider *why* you want to achieve a particular goal - what are your personal *reasons* underlying your desire for it? Having powerful reasons for achieving a goal can make a world of difference in your ability to achieve it - especially when the going gets tough.

Having *powerful reasons* for achieving a goal makes a world of difference in your ability to achieve it.

Let me share a couple of examples with you. At the Aikido Dojo that I attend there is a meek looking, petite woman who is about fifty years old. This woman is also a second Dan black belt, and is an incredible inspiration for us all, because she took up Aikido in her early forties, and maintained the discipline, courage and determination through injuries and setbacks, to attain not only a black belt, but her second Dan black belt - which could be likened to the difference between a Bachelor's degree and a Masters! When asked why she took up Aikido, and why she maintains her training, her reply was simple, yet very powerful: "I wanted to feel dangerous", she said! Here we have a small, middle aged woman who at first glance would be a pushover to even a teenage mugger - yet who in reality is a very dangerous woman indeed!

My own reason for taking up Aikido five years ago was that I was belted up quite badly. I want to be able to go anywhere, knowing I can handle myself. No one is ever going to touch me again!

Now that's a powerful reason, and any time my body is hurting, or I think the training is too hard, I just remember back to what it was like when I was attacked - and I train harder.

Finally, do *reward yourself when you achieve a goal*, or a significant milestone along the way to a goal. Even for small goals, give yourself a reward. If you give up cigarettes for a month, or even a week - be proud of the accomplishment. If you eat healthily, and limit your alcohol intake, then tell yourself you've done well today. See how many DFDs (Drug Free Days) you can put together in a row. Recognise that things like alcohol, coffee, cigarettes, and other so called 'recreational' drugs dull your senses, and blunt the keen edge needed to perform at your best. *They're for losers.*

Reward yourself when you achieve a goal.

Champions may not all be teetotallers, but I've rarely seen one that smokes, drinks to excess, or is addicted to coffee or marijuana. They also eat healthy food - recognising that their body is a superbly tuned engine, and their health is their greatest asset. You don't put cheap oil in a Rolls Royce engine, so don't put garbage food in *your* engine. Reduce meat, dairy products, and junk food, and eat more fresh fruit, cereals and vegetables.

Do something special, just for yourself, when you achieve a major goal; celebrate your successes, because this will build the motivation and confidence to go for the next goal, and the next. The more you set up a positive feedback loop, the more your system will want to continue to set goals, and achieve them. If you don't reward yourself, you won't build the positive goal setting habits that are a part of every champion's behaviour.

*"You are a champion because you live
with heart — having chosen your path,
you pursue it with gusto. "*

CHAPTER 4 :

PERSONAL POWER

MOTIVE IN ACTION

Motivation is the desire to do, to act, to expend energy toward the realisation of some goal or plan. It's also been described as *motive-in-action*. In other words, there are two parts to successful motivation: a clear *motive* or reason, and plenty of *action* or effort.

Lots of people have enough motive or desire for a particular dream, or cherished goal - but far fewer have learned how to take action on that motive; far fewer build the *entire* motivation to succeed. This ability to take action is a kind of power - your own *personal power*, and it could be said that there are only two kinds of people - those who have personal power, and those who don't.

Champions have developed both the motive, and learned how to consistently harness their ability to take action, to achieve their goals. Champions have *personal power*.

TAKING ACTION

I said in the previous chapter that true decisions are always followed by actions. If you make a true decision about something, it will always be followed by some positive action. Yet we see around us, the majority of people *not taking action* - not living up to their potential. Why not? What prevents them?

Why don't people take action? What prevents them?

I've identified six core reasons that stop people from being more successful in their life.

1. **They haven't set goals in the first place - so they have no reason, no motive, to act; or their goals don't adhere to the S.M.A.R.T.E.R. principles.**
2. **A lack of information or knowledge - so they can't develop a strategy to succeed.**
3. **The way they picture their goals prevents the goals from being compelling and positive.**
4. **The fear of failure - they fear that they will not succeed, and be ashamed - so they don't even try.**
5. **The fear of success - they fear the burdens of fame, responsibility, and fortune that success brings.**
6. **A low self esteem and self worth - their current self image is too small to allow great success.**

We dealt with the first problem in the last chapter, and the final three will be covered in the next few chapters, so let's turn our attention in the remainder of this chapter to how to develop a success strategy, and *compel* your goals.

PROGRAMMING FOR S.U.C.C.E.S.S.

Now I've been talking about personal power and taking action, but really, if you've set yourself a goal but not taken action toward it, then *you never really decided to go for the goal in the first place*! So the problem is not so much a lack of action, but rather a lack of a definite decision! It could be said that *personal power is the ability to make committed decisions,* rather than the ability to take action, because once you do make a definite decision, then you'll be compelled to act, automatically.

The following process, called the S.U.C.C.E.S.S. model, offers a way of getting to that decision point. It's modified from the work of Terry McClendon, to whom I am indebted for the acronym. The end result of the process is what is known in NLP as *a well formed outcome*, which not only identifies a specific goal, but also considers *how* to get it - a strategy for success.

Chris and Jules Collingwood describe a well formed outcome as:

"... like an opening gambit in chess. It sets up the scene for the rest of the game, and the level of attention given to plotting the outcome has a direct bearing on the ease with which desired results are achieved. A well formed outcome makes the difference between wanting something in theory, and becoming able to go and get it in practice..... A well formed outcome describes something that the user wants, in sensory based, positive terms. It includes a description of what the user wants if for, and the terms, conditions and environmental contexts in which the user want to have it. It includes consideration of different approaches to the outcome, and time frames, costs and consequences to interested parties, and whether it is within the user's control." (p. 1)

These S.U.C.C.E.S.S. principles are just as powerful whether you're dealing with a sports goal (eg. wanting to win an Olympic gold medal, become a professional golfer); a personal change issue (eg. wanting to give up smoking, lose weight); at work (eg. achieving a sales target; initiating new work practices); or for larger team and corporate projects (eg. winning the competition; achieving a production deadline; completing a merger operation).

The S.U.C.C.E.S.S. model can be used to design a positive strategy for sport, work, and personal issues.

The model has been modified from *McClendon & Associates'* NLP Practitioner Training Course, so please recognise that while this outline provides a useful introduction, mastery of the S.U.C.C.E.S.S. process does require professional training in NLP - in particular, meta-model questioning skills, which are essential information gathering tools needed to use the model correctly.

The S.U.C.C.E.S.S. model is particularly relevant to those aspiring to elite performance - I use it extensively in my work with elite athletes and sports teams, as well as with corporate clients. It is the *first step* I employ and I find it to be the *single most powerful tool* in fostering peak performance

Problems occur for both individuals and teams because they either 'don't know' what they really want, or they haven't taken the time to flesh out their desired outcome thoroughly enough so they can establish a viable achievement strategy.

Positive progress comes from identifying, describing, and committing to a desired positive outcome.

Identifying, describing and committing to a desired positive outcome is half the battle - and it's far easier to initiate and maintain positive progress and motivation in oneself, and in team members or employees, when there is a clear picture of where you're going and demonstrable progress steps along the way.

The S.U.C.C.E.S.S. model is described below as a practical seven-step procedure. Read through the steps, and *apply each of them to a current desired sport, personal or work situation*, experience how using them can foster a positive mindset for successful and rewarding improvement in that particular situation.

Apply each step to a current desired change situation.

Begin by asking yourself what positive changes do *you* want to achieve for yourself, or for your team or, organisation, in the next year or so? Pick something *you'd* like to change, do, learn, have, or be - individually, or as a team. Here are the steps:

S. STATED *POSITIVELY. I want to .....*
The first step is to elicit a *precise, positively stated* desired outcome. What is important here is to ensure that the goal is phrased in *positive* terms - ie. what you *want*, not what you want to avoid, or don't want.

For instance, someone stating a goal such as : 'I want to not get nervous before important matches', 'I don't want to go over budget', or 'I don't want to feel tired all the time', or 'I don't want to overeat', will want to rephrase them to be something like : 'I want to remain calm and confident before important matches', 'I want to stay under budget', or 'I want to feel alive and energetic', or 'I want to eat healthily'.

Clarity and *precision* are also important, and goals such as : 'I want to lose weight', or 'I want to be a better speaker', or 'I want to be more successful', or 'I want to get fitter', require further clarification, such as : 'I want to maintain a trim build and weight of 74kg', or 'I want to prepare and rehearse my talks well, and hold eye contact with the audience when I speak', or 'I want to be promoted to such-and-such a position', or 'I want to be fit enough to complete a triathlon'.

State what you *want*, not what you *don't* want.

U. UNDENIABLE REALITY : *I know this to be true when ..... (sensory-based description)*

The next step is to identify *how you will know when you have achieved the goal or change you want*, emphasising a *sensory-based* description of this knowledge. While this might at first seem obvious, it becomes a little more challenging when dealing with desired emotional states or behaviours. Consequently, it becomes necessary to identify in *sensory specific terms*, precisely what you, or the team, will see, hear and feel when you will have achieved the desired outcome.

Identify the desired outcome in *sensory specific terms*.

An example of a desired change to the attitude of a sports team or work group might be: 'We see all the players arriving early, training enthusiastically, and getting on well together; we hear individual team members saying how good it is to play for this club; and we feel a sense of determination and hungriness to win from the players when competing.'

A simple personal example for achieving a desired weight goal might be : 'I see the bathroom scales reading 74kg when I step onto them; I feel light and energetic; and I hear my friends and work colleagues telling me how great I'm looking'.

An example of a change to your sales manner might be : 'I hear myself with a helpful, polite tone to the customers; I picture myself providing a high standard of service which exceeds their expectations, and I imagine them smiling and content; and I feel relaxed and confident, and the satisfaction of being truly helpful.'

Identify the *specific behaviours* you want.

This is a really important step, because you will identify the *specific behaviours* you want in either yourself or your staff in order to achieve success. Too often in desired change situations the emphasis is placed on just the outcome, rather than *the means by which you will achieve the outcome* - and it's the *process* that provides the specific information and direction for you to follow.

C. CONTEXTS : *The places and times I want this are .....*
The next step is to identify *in what specific situations and contexts you want to experience these specific behaviours.*

Some examples might be: 'when we're losing, and under pressure', or 'when a potential customer telephones, or walks in the door', or 'when I'm confronted by an angry staff member', or 'when I'm offered unhealthy, sweet rolls at morning tea'.

Identify where you want to have these behaviours.

C. CONGRUENT WITH PERSONAL VALUES : *I want this because* .....

The next step is to ensure that the desired outcome is in line with your individual personal values and / or team or corporate mission statement and goals.

Sometimes, a person can want something that either goes against another strongly held value, or they may want it for a self destructive reason - for instance, someone wanting to follow a strict dietary regimen 'to punish myself', or to play well to 'knock so-and-so out of the running', or to achieve a particular level of productivity 'to show up the deficiencies of another department', none of which are acceptable reasons.

> **Asking *for what purpose* the desired outcome is, ensures you work toward positive, constructive goals.**

Asking *for what purpose,* ensures that you work toward positive, constructive goals that are in harmony with your core values and beliefs. An example from someone who is aiming for a higher sports performance might be : 'I want it because it will give me a feeling of satisfaction and self worth'. An example from someone wanting to improve their telephone manner might be : 'I want it because it will increase my sales, and help advance my career.'

E. ECOLOGICAL : *Does any part of me or the organisation object to being / doing / having this?*

This step is to check that the desired change is in harmony with all 'parts' of you, and / or all departments of your organisation. This was discussed in detail in the previous chapter, and is a simple check to ensure that there is no inner resistance from yourself, or outer resistance from others, to the desired changes.

This is important, as one of the main reasons for 'backsliding' in effecting positive behavioural change, is that if there is a 'part' of the individual or organisation that doesn't really want to change, then it may sabotage the process.

Recognise that it is *usual to have some objections*. This makes sense when you think about it, because the status quo is usually *perceived* as doing something of a positive nature for the individual or group. When you come across objections, the trick is to identify the *positive intention* behind the objection, and find at least *three other effective ways* of achieving the same intention.

If you come across objections, identify the *positive intention* behind the objection.

For example, a common positive intention behind smoking is that smoking currently gives the person a way of feeling relaxed and at ease, so in changing you would want to develop three or four *other ways* of feeling relaxed and at ease. Or a common positive intention behind emotional outbursts or confrontations on the field is the desire to stand up for yourself, so to change you would want to find three or four other ways of being assertive.

Likewise, a common positive intention for being reluctant to make sales calls, is that it provides the person with a sense of safety - you can't 'fail' at making a sale if you don't make the call, and so you would want to teach your staff three or four *other ways* of feeling safe and confident when making sales calls.

It's recommended that at least three other behaviours are provided for the person or group to allow them a *range of choice* in selecting how they want to behave in a given context.

S. SELF INITIATED AND MAINTAINED : *How can I take charge of doing this myself?*

The next step is to ensure that you, or the group, can initiate and maintain the desired change or outcome. The most effective, positive changes occur when the responsibility for that change comes from within the individual or organisation themselves, rather than being imposed from outside. So efforts directed toward establishing *self control of the new behaviours* are essential to the S.U.C.C.E.S.S. process.

An example of how this can be done for someone who wants to control pre-performance anxiety in sport, the performing arts, or public speaking might be : 'Develop a pre-performance mental routine of visualising and thinking about the desired positive outcome - how I want to perform. Stop negative self talk, and use a confident posture, movements and emotional triggers to generate positive states prior to the performances'.

Establish the old behaviour as the trigger for beginning the new one.

Another helpful hint is to *establish the old behaviour as the trigger for beginning the new one*! So the old feeling of desire for a cigarette, now becomes a trigger to engage in some deep breaths or a quick walk to relax and let go of stress. The old feeling of anger and loss of control over a poor umpiring decision now becomes the trigger for strong determination to concentrate, play harder, and hunger to win. The old feeling of nervousness and unconfidence about dealing with an angry staff member or customer now becomes the trigger for active listening to their grievance, building positive rapport, and feeling confident about finding a positive solution.

S. STRATEGY : *What steps do I need to take in order to achieve the desired outcome?*

The final step in the process is to develop an *action plan* - what do I need to do today, tomorrow, next week, next month, over the next year, and so on, to achieve the outcome?

You want to have a *strategy* for achieving your goals.

A good example has been my establishment of the *Sportsmind* Institute - as a strategy for building a network of 1,000 NLP trained coaches / sports trainers around the world. My first step was to research the latest ideas and techniques in Psychological Skills Training in sport, and the mental and emotional preparation techniques of top coaches and athletes around the world - and add NLP techniques. I did this under the umbrella of a Master of Science degree - to provide my work with scientific credibility and substance. I also aspired to *practical credibility* by taking up Aikido, and setting a personal goal to achieve my black belt.

I wrote and self published the *Sportsmind* book and audio tapes, and undertook extensive promotional and speaking tours around Australia to promote my work. From these tours and media interviews, I established an extensive network of sportspeople on a mailing list, and wrote a regular newsletter to provide these people with information and ideas, as well as details of *Sportsmind* products and workshops. I also linked up with the NSW Dept. of Sport, who assisted with organising numerous *Sportsmind* workshops throughout the state.

Finally, I designed the *Sportsmind* Correspondence and NLP Practitioner programs and have begun training interested people. I have a web site, and write articles for sport / fitness magazines.

CASE STUDY : Veterans Tennis player

The following example is of a Veterans tennis player, with whom I used the S.U.C.C.E.S.S. model, so you can see and hear how it works in practice to establish a clearly defined, positive outcome.

STATED POSITIVELY : *I want to - feel confident and relaxed; determined and aggressive; to produce my best; to be positive, at ease and looking forward to it; and sleep well the night before a match.*

UNDENIABLE REALITY : *I know this to be true when -*
Feelings .... I feel taller; relaxed around my shoulders with even breathing; I experience a sense of strength throughout my whole body; I move in a way that shows I mean business and am on a mission; there is a warmth over my whole body; and my facial muscles are content.
Seeing .... I clearly see everything around me; and I picture myself doing what I'd like to do successfully. The pictures are in front of me about 5 - 6 meters away, bigger than life and in dynamic lifelike colour, bright and with movement and action.
Hearing .... I hear all the sounds around me, and experience internal silence.

CONTEXTS : *The places and times I want this are -*
 # Before major tennis events - state or national titles.
 # When I'm in a new environment - eg new playing venues.
 # When I have to play someone I don't know.
 # If I'm given a new task and deadline by my boss.
 # When driving in the city - especially at peak hour.
 # When I meet and converse with new people who are potential friends / acquaintances.
[Note: these last three were not related to tennis. It's common for someone to include other contexts or situations]

CONGRUENT : *I want this because* - *I want to achieve more and do it with ease to give me a feeling of satisfaction and contentment and self worth.*

ECOLOGICAL : *Does any part of me object to being / doing / having this?* - *No.*

SELF INITIATED : *Can I take charge of doing this myself?* - *Yes.*

STRATEGY : *How can I do this?*
A number of Sportsmind sessions with Jeffrey Hodges, work through the six week program in the back of the Sportsmind book, and do the visualisation exercises on the tapes daily.

We further clarified the outcome by using the SMARTER goal setting principles, which resulted in :

6 Month Goals
* To be in control of my emotions before and during tennis matches. I want to feel confident, relaxed, and aggressive.
* To have this same control of my emotions in other areas of my life: especially when I am around new people who are potential friends; when given a new task and deadline by my boss; and when driving in the city.
* To win 3 events I enter in at the local tournament next month.

12 Month - 2 year Goals
* To win a major Veterans tournament next year.
* To attend Wimbledon in 1999.

3 - 5 year Goals
* To be selected in the Australian team for the World Veterans Titles for tennis.

CASE STUDY : Olympic Kayaker

Here's another example, with just the first two steps, to show the importance of obtaining a positively stated, *sensory based description* of the desired outcome.

STATED POSITIVELY : *I want to -*

1. *"I want to be planned the whole way to Gold Medal in the K2 or K4 at the Olympics in Sydney 2000."*
2. *"I want to emit an aura of CONFIDENCE in what I am doing at all times - even when I have a set back along the way. I want to do the work - even when it's hard. I want to be mentally prepared to enjoy the hard work."*

UNDENIABLE REALITY : *I know this to be true when -*

1. *I have a skeleton training plan to 2000, including a written plan of my mental state and decision points on the way. A master plan in the office on the wall and an enlarged photo, framed of the one I currently have on my bedside.*

2. *Hearing .... I am relaxed in my thoughts. I know what to do. I hear my husband saying "You've done the work, now go out there and hit the front and win!", and say to myself "You've done the work, now enjoy everything. It'll take care of itself because you've done the work. It's now how much you want it."*
Seeing .... External visual focus, with everything looking vivid and bright. An awareness of the crowd, and surroundings.
Feelings .... Energy in solar plexus which moves up to the chest, and relaxes into my head. A warmth up my neck and over my face. Strong posture, and a feeling of strength in my shoulders. Face relaxed, with a natural smile. My arms and legs are relaxed and energised. No feeling of a need to move very much, and doing what I need to do at the right times. A feeling of doing it for other people - for my husband, and the crowd.

EXERCISE : Using the S.U.C.C.E.S.S. Process

Now it's *your* turn. Use the seven steps of the S.U.C.C.E.S.S. process now to identify and design a well formed outcome and a positive achievement strategy for yourself.

STATED POSITIVELY : *I want to -* _____

_____

_____

UNDENIABLE REALITY : *I know this to be true when -*
    Feelings : _____
    Seeing : _____
    Hearing : _____

CONTEXTS : *The places and times I want this are -*

_____

_____

CONGRUENT : *I want this because -*

_____

_____

ECOLOGICAL : *Does any part of me object to being / doing / having this? -*

_____

SELF INITIATED : *Can I take charge of doing this myself?*

_____

STRATEGY : *How can I do this?*

_____

_____

POSITIVE COMPULSIONS

I mentioned earlier that one of the reasons why people don't take action, is that the way they picture their goals prevents those goals from being *compelling* and attractive. Yet these same people have no problem acting on negative 'goals' such as smoking, over-eating chocolate, emotional 'reactions', and so on. One of the reasons for this is that these negative *compulsions* are pictured and experienced by the person very differently.

> **The way you picture something affects how *compelling* and attractive it is, and how you act toward it.**

Compulsions are only compulsions because of the way you picture, hear and feel them! What if you had a *compulsion* for positive behaviours and empowering emotional states? The difference between a champion and an average person is simply that they have chosen different things to focus on and get excited about - they have compulsions for positive behaviours like eating healthily, fitness training, and feeling good about themselves, instead of smoking, overeating, sloth and feeling lousy!

But what makes a compulsion, compelling? Why do some people just *have to* have a cigarette, or eat chocolate, or go surfing, bite their fingernails, or get anxious at the sight of a spider? We act on compulsions as a result of the *structure* of our subjective experience, the structure of *how* we think about a particular thing.

> **Champions have compulsions for positive behaviours and empowering emotional states.**

SUBMODALITIES AND THE STRUCTURE OF THINKING

I noted in the first chapter that the NLP model postulates that every behaviour is a consequence of our thinking - and our thinking is made up of seeing images, hearing sounds or words, and feelings, smells, and tastes. Everything we do is a result of using these five sensory thinking components - and in particular, the three primary senses of seeing, hearing, and feeling.

However, each of these primary sensory systems also includes numerous *submodalities* - which are finer distinctions or refinements of that sensory system. For instance, our visual sense has the submodalities of colour, size, brightness, distance, shape, and so on. Our auditory sense has the submodalities of volume, tone, tempo, distance, and so on.

By varying the submodalities of a particular thought, you can totally change your response to it.

Submodalities are really important aspects of our thinking, because by varying the submodalities of a particular thought, even only slightly, you can totally change your response to it. For instance, if you want to be more motivated, or compelled, to achieve a particular goal or outcome, then picture, hear and feel about that outcome in the same way that you picture, hear and feel about something you're *absolutely compelled* to do.

If you think of a desired goal, and 'see' it in full colour, big and bright, large, and up close directly in front of you; and say to yourself in a loud, confident voice "YES! I want this, now!"; and feel an excitement welling up within you, and a tingling all over your body - that's pretty hard to resist!

In contrast, if you 'see' a goal dim, fuzzy, and distant; say to yourself in an unsure tone of voice "I hope I get this"; and feel unsure and cool, then you're probably not going to have much 'go for it'!

Generally, for most people, visual submodalities of compulsion are: large size, close, colourful, 3-D, bright and moving. Auditory compelling submodalities are louder, stereo sounds or voices, close, with resonant tone. Kinaesthetic, (or feeling), submodalities of compulsion are warmer, faster movement, higher intensity and strong rhythm.

However, there can be individual differences. Do the following exercise to identify the submodalitites that are compelling for you.

EXERCISE : Submodalities of Compulsion

1. Think of something you're really *compelled* to do. A favourite pastime, something you do if you get half a chance. For example it might be an activity like going to the beach, or tinkering with your motorbike, or maybe a favourite TV program you never miss. [Use a *positive* activity - something you enjoy doing and is not unhealthy or self destructive]

2. Now think of that activity, and as you think of it, notice the visual, auditory and kinaesthetic submodalities of your thoughts. How do you picture the activity? What and how do you talk to yourself about it? And your feelings?

3. Now think of something that you'd *like* to be more motivated, or compelled to do. Imagine doing it using the same visual, auditory and kinaesthetic submodalities you use for your compulsive activity.

TIMELINES

Timelines are another important aspect of your thinking processes that can affect your ability to take action. Essentially a timeline is an individual's way of organising time in their mind, and it's quite usual for there to be significant differences in the way different people think about time.

Everyone I've come across distinguishes differences in time by using *relative positions in space.* If you think about it, we have to have a way of knowing the difference between, say an experience that happened to us just yesterday, and something that happened a month ago, or a year ago. Likewise, we think about an event that is expected to happen tomorrow, differently from six months time, and differently again for an event five years from now.

> **Timelines are ways of organising time in our mind - we distinguish differences in time by using *relative positions in space.***

For example, a simple timeline might have the near past just behind the person, and the more distant past going progressively further away behind them in a line. Their future may be represented as a line directly in front of them, or perhaps on a slight diagonal, with the near future close and the more distant future getting progressively further away from the person.

Other common timelines have the past in a line to the person's left, and the future to their right, or vice versa; or past and future going out in a 'V' shape from the person. Timelines can also go up, or down, or curve, but most commonly they're fairly straight.

I've described timelines, (and submodalities), in more detail in the *Sportsmind* book - including a simple exercise for identifying your own timeline - so I encourage you to find more information there if you're interested.

The significance of timelines is that, like submodalities, they can be used to either empower you and enhance your performance, or they can limit you and hold you back from realising your potential.

Timelines can be used to empower you and enhance your performance - or limit you.

For instance, some people might set goals, and even picture them with compelling submodalities - but they forget to put that picture in their future, or they don't place it actually *on* their future timeline. Consequently, when they look into the future, they can't see themselves having achieved the goal.

Likewise, individuals who have their future way off to the right or left, rather than in front of them, tend to be less motivated - because the goals are 'over there' rather than right in their face in front of them. All the most motivated people I know have their future pretty much directly in front of them - and one person I know has her future in front, on a downward slant! Life is always easy for her - it's all a down hill run!

Try that yourself. Imagine your future timeline, and now tilt it downward slightly. Doesn't it make things seem easier? Do the reverse for a moment - tilt it upwards. Seems like you're going uphill doesn't it? Realise that little things like this can make a real difference to your experience - and to your motivation!

Also, how extended is your timeline? Some people have really huge timelines, with tomorrow about ten meters away, next week is over the road, and to even consider seeing a year in the future they'd have to be on a football oval to fit it in!

Conversely, some people have their timelines so squashed up that tomorrow, next year and twenty years from now are all within less than a meter away from them! Blink, and there goes their life - it's that short!

> **Your experience of time - it's duration - depends on how extended or contracted your timeline is!**

Again, try out changing *your* timeline like the above two for a few minutes - what do you experience? When your timeline is really extended, you feel like you've got all the time in the world, and when it's all pushed together you feel rushed! Isn't it so?

Another interesting thing about timelines that I've discovered is that really top sportspeople make distinctions about positive and negative past events and store them in different places, sometimes even on separate timelines! They put the poor performances and 'failures' *behind them*, while the good performances and victories are usually stored somewhere close, either to the side or in front.

The advantage of this way of differentiating 'bad' and 'good' events is that the negative events are quickly forgotten, while the positive ones can be used to continually build confidence and motivation. Try it yourself. Think of all the successes you've had, now gather them up together and put them in a spot say, just a bit to your left and in front of you. Any negative experiences put in a line behind you. It changes how you feel, doesn't it?

The really good news is that submodalities, timelines, and all the other aspects of your internal thinking processes are under *your* control - so if you're using a timeline that's not as effective as another, you can change it!

> **Submodalities, timelines, and all the aspects of your internal thinking processes are under *your* control.**

So put your timeline back to where it normally is - or perhaps you might want to explore using a different timeline for a little while. If so, recognise that it can be a little disorienting at first!

Now that you know about submodalities and timelines, you can use them to *compel your future* with the following exercise :

EXERCISE : Creating a *Compelling* Future

1. Identify a <u>positive</u> compulsion, and note submodalities.
2. Build a slide and soundtrack of a desired goal using these.
3. Identify future timeline, flatten, and flag key future dates.
4. Place slide onto timeline at desired date. Ecology check - does any part of me object to achieving this goal?
5. <u>Physically</u> walk future timeline, associate into goal, and note feelings. Look into future from here. Ecology check.
6. Walking <u>backwards</u> bring a <u>small bit</u> of the feeling back with you to present. [You want to feel a pull towards goal]
7. Notice other things that will be required prior to achieving the goal, and add these in. Take observer perspectives - look down on your timeline, from the left, and the right.
8. Lock the goal into place. Return timeline to normal.

CASE STUDIES : Motivation to exercise; business goal.

I've worked with literally hundreds of people using the above technique, all with outstanding results. The two most memorable were a woman who was having trouble motivating herself to exercise regularly, and a man who had a business goal to open up some retail stores. I used the woman's positive compulsion of loving to see a favourite actor in a movie to elicit her compelling submodalities, the most significant of which were big, bright, colourful, moving pictures. Once she pictured herself exercising with these submodalities, and the positive outcome on her figure and health, she was able to maintain a regular training program.

The businessman was interesting in that his positive compulsion was to call his mother regularly and talk with her - what a wonderful thing to be compelled to do regularly! Again, his most significant submodalities of compulsion were big, bright, colourful, moving pictures, and we were able to program in his goals very powerfully, which he then achieved as planned.

One other example I can relate is of my writing *Sportsmind*. In January 1993 I did not have a single word of the book written, I just knew I wanted to write it. So I went through the above exercise with a friend of mine who is also an NLP Master Practitioner, placing a compelling picture of myself with the completed book in my hand in September that year on my timeline. Following the exercise I was so motivated to write that I completed writing it by June, went to the printers and had it self published for release in September, right on deadline!

The key to making the exercise work is to *fully associate* into the goal as achieved at the future time, and to withdraw just a taste of that feeling back to the present with you, leaving the rest of the feeling there - almost like a rubber band being stretched from the future, back to the present. This is what provides the motivation.

"You are a champion because you stay happy — even when things don't work out, your joyful natue is a powerful influence."

CHAPTER 5 :

CHAMPION FEELINGS

IMPORTANCE OF FEELINGS

Feelings are important to success.

Your performance at work; in your relationships; in education; in sport; and in every other area of your life, is profoundly influenced by your *feelings*, isn't it? How you *feel* affects how well you perform.

Your emotional states influence your thinking, your behaviour, your tone of voice, your posture, and even your health.

But feelings don't 'just happen' to you - feelings are *choices*. Champions recognise this and choose their feelings. Feelings that empower them, and allow them to fully utilise their physical prowess and mental skills.

Champions have learned how to *choose* the states they live in.

HOW MANY GOOD FEELINGS DO YOU HAVE ?

Let me ask you a question: How many *good* feelings do you have? And how much time in a day do you spend feeling good?

Likewise, how many *bad* feelings can you identify ..... and how much time do you spend in a day feeling bad?

Think about it for a minute.

Many people spend more time in the day feeling bad, than they do *actively feeling good feelings!*

If you're like a lot of people, you will probably only be able to think of a few good feelings - but lots of bad ones! For instance, a *short list* of bad feelings might run like this:

Worried; Depressed; Sad; Frustrated; Unconfident; Uptight; Angry; Tired; Tense; Bad; Embarrassed; Pressured; Jealous; Anxious; Unmotivated; Lonely; Weak; Victimised; Sorry-for-self; Nervous; Powerless; Self righteous; Apathetic; Trapped; Unloved; Pitiful; Heavy; Procrastinating; Lousy; Vindictive; Down; Put-upon; Rushed; Sick; Tentative; Bashful; Grumpy; Hesitant; Confused; Stressed; Uncertain; Uncreative; Pensive; Lost; Betrayed; Itchy; Spaced-out; In Crisis; Directionless; Stuck; Impatient; Hurt; Unprepared; Clumsy; Bored; Sullen; Slow; Fragile; Un-coordinated; Guilty; Greedy; Anguished; Fearful; Selfish; Regretful; Grieving; Isolated; Withdrawn; and Sleepy .... to name just a *few*!

I think that many people spend more time in the day feeling either bad, or neutral, than they do *actively feeling good feelings!*

CHAMPION FEELINGS

What do *champions* feel? How do they use their emotional states to generate excellence in themselves? What *champion feelings* do they choose?

I've listed some below that I've identified in peak performers. Perhaps you can think of others. Why not choose, right now, to experience one of the following *champion feelings* :

* **Joy - a feeling of intense happiness**
* **Enthusiasm - a feeling of being fully alive and energised**
* **Purpose - a feeling of certainty and direction in your life**
* **Determination - a feeling of being fully committed to a task or goal**
* **Courage - a feeling of strength in the face of adversity or risk**
* **Focus - a feeling of pinpoint concentration**
* **Love - a feeling of caring, and giving of yourself**
* **Adventure - a feeling of excitement and challenge**
* **Momentum - a feeling of moving to a destination**
* **Belonging - a feeling of connection to others**
* **Balance - a feeling of centred control of self**
* **Timing - a feeling of being in perfect sync with outside forces**
* **Power - a feeling of energy to achieve an outcome**
* **Serenity - a feeling of supreme peace and contentment**
* **Gratefulness - a feeling of appreciation and thanks**
* **Empathy - a feeling of understanding/sharing with others**
* **Satisfaction - a feeling of recognition/reward for effort**
* **Conviction - a feeling of certainty of direction or opinion**
* **Mortality - a feeling of sharpness and clarity that comes only from a sense of one's impending, inevitable death**

Every instant, you're creating or manufacturing *some* kind of feeling - whether it be a negative feeling like indifference, anger, depression, sullenness, apathy or unconfidence; or a positive feeling like joy, confidence, enthusiasm, excitement, conviction, or some of the others I've listed above.

Every instant, you're creating *some* kind of feeling.

The trouble is, that many people simply *don't recognise, or label, their feeling states.* As a consequence, their behaviour is being directed unconsciously - by feelings they are not even aware of! Because your behaviour is profoundly affected by your feelings, if you don't really know or are aware of what you're feeling - how can you be in charge of your behaviour, or your performances?

In order to be in charge of your personal performance, in any area of life, *you want to be aware of your feeling states, and maintain that awareness from moment to moment.*

To perform well, you want to be aware of your feelings and maintain that awareness from moment to moment.

Take a moment, right now, and recognise what you're feeling - right now, right this instant! What are you feeling, right now, as you read these words?

Don't dismiss the question, or dodge the answer by saying "I'm feeling 'OK' or 'all right', or 'nothing'", or "I don't know". *Find out!* Get in touch with yourself, with your feelings, and describe what you're currently experiencing. Put a label on your feelings.

LABELLING YOUR FEELINGS

It's important to label your feelings. If you don't put labels on them you'll find them difficult to change if they're negative, and you also won't understand what is directing your behaviours!

If you don't label your feelings you won't be able to understand what is directing your behaviours!

Once you've identified a feeling or emotional state, then you can go about changing it if it's disempowering or counter-productive. In addition, if it's a positive and useful feeling or emotional state, then you can *actively enhance and amplify it* and make it even more effective and powerful in your life.

I think it's so important to have a *vocabulary of champion feelings* - because if you can't conceptualise or put a name to a feeling, how can you ever experience it? If you don't identify a feeling, then you won't ever feel it - consciously, or understand what it is that you're feeling, and how to use it. *If a feeling is not in your language, then you won't make use of it in your life.*

If a feeling is not in your language, then you won't make use of it in your life.

Why impoverish yourself by limiting your range of positive emotions to just a few? Practice experiencing all the champion feelings that I've listed, and actively use them in your life. Take a few minutes now to go through the list, and *feel* them one at a time, and think of places where you could use them.

CHOOSING POSITIVE FEELINGS AND EMOTIONS

I believe it's possible to only experience positive, empowering feelings in your life - if you want.

There's a lot of garbage been spouted by the psychological fraternity that encourages the 'expression' of negative emotions in order to 'release' them. However the expression of a negative emotion, *actually reinforces it*, rather than 'releases' it.

The expression of a negative emotion *reinforces it*!

This makes sense when you understand that every behaviour - whether it be a feeling state, a thought, or a physical action - is a result of a specific neurological circuit that fires in the brain. The more you do a certain behaviour, or feel a feeling, the easier it is to do it again - you actually 'groove in' the behaviour or emotion, neurologically. So 'emotional release' therapy, in my opinion, actually reinforces the behaviours it purports to change!

There is also a body of opinion which suggests that 'one has to know the negative in order to fully appreciate and experience the positive'. That one has to 'accept' negative emotions as part and parcel of being human. What a load of rubbish! That's like saying you've got to become a cripple in order to learn how to walk properly, or you've got to experience stuttering in order to learn how to be a great orator!

Our challenge is to learn to reframe and transform negative emotions - not 'accept' them.

Of course we all experience negative emotions and feelings from time to time, but our challenge is to learn to reframe them, and transform them - not 'accept' them. We want to learn to *respond differently* to whatever it was that triggered the negative response in future - not reinforce the negative states by 'accepting them', or justifying them.

Learn to *respond differently* to whatever it was that triggered the negative feeling or emotion.

You don't have to feel sadness in order to understand and feel happy. You don't have to first hate in order to know love. And you certainly don't need to fully experience depression and apathy to feel and express enthusiasm, vitality, and joie de vivre!

You don't need to experience depression and apathy to feel and express enthusiasm and joie de vivre!

I think the confusion for psychologists and others has grown out of not distinguishing one's *feelings* from one's *self*. Because of the importance of encouraging *self acceptance*, (a worthwhile and desirable goal with which I concur), there has been a tendency for this self acceptance to spill over into accepting behaviours, attitudes, thoughts and feelings far below our potential - negative thoughts, mediocre behaviours, destructive attitudes, and disempowering feelings and emotions.

Your feelings are not your self. Accept yourself, but be discriminating about which feelings you accept.

Accepting such mediocrity has no place in someone aiming for excellence and champion status in their life. Certainly accept and like *yourself,* this is in fact essential, but reject mediocrity. Reject negative, disempowering or destructive feelings in yourself!

Of course, this doesn't mean that you will never experience negative emotions again, or that they don't have *some* positive use or meaning in our lives. Negative feelings such as anger, frustration, envy, loneliness, boredom, sadness, or whatever, want to be seen to be *calls to action* - messages from yourself that something is wrong and you need to *do* something about it!

Negative feelings want to be seen to be *calls to action*.

But they want to be *immediately acted upon* rather than stewed over! The trouble with negative feelings is that people just get stuck in them, and then don't know how to get out! A negative feeling is a call to change yourself, or the situation, in some way - because you're in pain! Once you recognise the message behind the negative feeling, and taken the action, you can let it go! Why would you want to hang on to it - who honestly *likes* to feel bad?

Negative states can also become positive resources in the right contexts. What if you used a feeling of procrastination for bad feelings - what if you just never got around to feeling them, you just kept putting them off! Or you could use a feeling of impatience anytime you want to feel more motivated to achieve your goals. Or what if you felt hesitant or fearful every time you were offered cigarettes or junk food - you just couldn't do it!

Negative states can be resources in the right contexts.

EMOTIONAL STATES ARE CHOICES

Of course, you would understand that your performance at work; in your relationships; in education; in sport; and so on, is profoundly influenced by your *feelings*, isn't it? How you *feel* affects how well you perform.

Your emotional states influence your thinking, your behaviour, your tone of voice, your posture, and even your health. Negative emotions foster dis-ease in the body and stress in the mind. Positive emotions energise the body and mind, encourage the production of endorphins and other peak performance hormones, and boost your immune system.

Emotional states influence your thinking, behaviour, tone of voice, posture, and even your health.

But states don't just jump on you out of the blue do they? You don't suddenly experience violent rage, intense loneliness, or delirious happiness for no reason do you? Feelings don't 'just happen' to you - feelings are *choices*.

States are *effects* - they're a result of things you're doing in your mind. In fact, it could be said that every behaviour, or feeling, has to happen first in your mind, before it happens in your body. States are also *processes*, they're not static - you change 'state' regularly throughout the day don't you? So confidence, anger, motivation, unconfidence and all the other positive and negative emotions are *dynamic processes* - something is going on to create them. All states are dynamic, not static. Confidence is a process, not a static state; motivation is a process, not a static state; enthusiasm is a process, not a static state.

BUILDING BLOCKS OF STATE

So let's look at and explore how you create feeling states in yourself, and how this can affect your performance. There are two questions about state that are important: Firstly, *what states* are most useful for success in *your* sport or work?; and secondly, how can we deliberately create those states in ourselves?

How do we create states in ourselves?

Stop for a few minutes, and answer these questions for *your* situation: What states lead to success in my sport / work? And, how do I build those states in myself?

What states did you think of? Some examples of states that top sportspeople usually mention are: Relaxed; Confident; Positive; Focused; Determined; Aggressive; and Hungry to Win. Feeling a sense of Enjoyment, and Happiness or Fun when playing also rates highly for most successful sportspeople.

However, few people ever answer the second question - how do I create those states in myself? This is because, for many people, their state is not under conscious control. They just 're-act' to external circumstances and situations rather than choosing a state that would be most useful to them in a given context, and *deliberately building that state in themselves*, prior to performing. They just leave their state to chance, and 'hope' to do well. This isn't good enough.

Many people 're-act' to external circumstances and situations rather than choosing their state.

It's important to know how to create states in yourself, so you can manage your state .... so you can deliberately build the most resourceful and capable states in yourself *before* you even step onto the playing field, tennis court, golf course, podium, business meeting, stage, or wherever *you* perform.

So what are the 'building blocks' of state? What answers did you come up with for the second question?

I've identified *three* building blocks of state, and whatever answers you came up with, you'll probably find that they fit into one of the following three categories : Physiology; Ideology; and Environment.

There are three building blocks of state :
Physiology; Ideology; and Environment.

The building blocks of state are your *physiology* - or body posture, breathing, movements, and facial expressions; your *ideology* - or what you're imagining, and saying to yourself; and the *environment* around you - or everything else outside of yourself, including both the physical and social environments.

Lets look at each of these in more detail now.

<u>Physiology</u>. It's easy to recognise how our physiology - our body posture, breathing, facial expressions, and the way we move - affects our state. For example, think how differently you feel if you hang your head, breath shallowly, slouch, and slowly shuffle around .... compared to holding your head up high, breathe deeply with an erect posture, put a smile on your face, and move quickly.

How is your state *right now*? Are you feeling energised and enthusiastic about your life, and about your sport or work? If you're not, try changing your physiology *now*. You can change how you feel, quickly and easily simply by changing how you move, how you breathe, your facial expressions, and how you hold your head.

Interestingly, it's been discovered that simply *smiling*, activates a lot of positive emotional and hormonal 'circuits' in the body - and is extremely beneficial for your health!

Take a few moments *right now* and stand up straight .... take five deep breaths .... smile, and walk briskly around the room. Stop reading and do this exercise now!

Welcome back. Did it make a difference to how you're feeling? It's a simple thing, but changing your physiology is one of the quickest and easiest ways to change your state, isn't it?

**Changing your physiology is one of the quickest
and easiest ways to change your state.**

One of the best examples of how physiology affects performance was told to me by a tennis coach who had taken a group of Australian teenagers to compete in some tournaments in the USA. He noted how the Australians, when they went out to shake hands at the beginning of the games, slouched out with their head and eyes down, while the Americans walked out with an erect posture, head up, eyes directly on their opponent.

Needless to say, the Australian players all underperformed, while the Americans all played confidently and consistently!

<u>Ideology</u>.   Your ideology is the combination of what you're imagining and saying to yourself in your mind - and again, this has a powerful impact on your state. For instance, for someone to feel *nervous and unconfident* about asking someone out on a date, what kinds of things would they imagine? What would they say to themselves?

If you imagined being rejected, or worse still, laughed at when you asked them out, and you said to yourself "Oh, they'll never want to go out with me ... I'm not interesting enough", it's easy to see how you could quickly create a negative state, isn't it?

Now relate this concept to your sport or work. Think of a time you were performing really well, and were feeling confident and focused. What kinds of things were you saying to yourself? What did you imagine? Why not do these things *deliberately* to create the kinds of positive states you want to experience in your sport or work, every time you play?

What *could* you imagine and say to yourself to create more positive states for yourself?

What could you imagine and say to yourself to create more confidence? More hungriness to win? More relaxed and positive states? What could you imagine and say to yourself to feel more enjoyment in your training and competition, or at work?

It's important to also recognise that it's not just *what* you say, or imagine, that affects your state, but also *how* you imagine the pictures, and *how* you hear the words. It's not only the *content* of words and images, that you use, but also the specific *submodalities* of each that affect your state.

You will recall that I introduced the concept of submodalities in the last chapter, and I explained how for most people a goal can be made more compelling if it is pictured big, bright, colourful, and up close. In the same way, the specific visual and auditory submodalities you use in your thinking about *anything* will affect your state.

> **It's not just *what* you say, or imagine, that affects your state, but also the specific *submodalities* you use.**

For example, I'm sure you have at one time or another, criticised yourself for something ... a silly mistake, an oversight, a poor performance, whatever. Take a moment to recall that critical voice, and as you do, notice the *direction* it comes from. Do you experience it from your left or right, from in front of or behind you? How *far away* is the voice - does it seem close, or far away? How *loud* is the voice, and what is its *tone* like?

Now, just as a bit of an experiment, change each of those submodalities and hear your voice say the same thing in a different way. For instance, if the voice seems to come from just behind your left ear, up close ..... then move it further away, and hear it coming from out in front of you. If the voice is loud, make it softer. If it has a high pitched, whining tone .... change it to be a deep throaty voice.

What happens when you do this?

It's hard to still feel lousy when your internal critic sounds like a sultry paramour out in front of you, doesn't it. I mean, if you're going to critique your performance, why not have it sound like Tina Turner or Demi Moore?

Likewise, if you have a poor performance and you continue to picture that up close, big, bright and right in front of you .... how do you think it will affect your state? Or if you put in a personal best performance, and you remember that as a tiny, black and white, postage stamp sized picture, behind you .... how much effect will that have on your state?

The quality of your *external* experience is directly related to the quality of your *internal* experience.

One of the consistent things I've found in all champion performers - whether they be athletes, or business people - is that they do just the opposite to this. Champions remember their good performances as big, colourful, bright pictures, up close in front of them. And of course, this gives them the confidence to attempt their next big goal - and succeed. Remember, the quality of your *external* experience is directly related to the quality of your *internal* experience.

When they have an off day, they let it go by seeing it small, and dim, and they deliberately push it away, and out behind them so it no longer affects them.

Every negative state has a mental structure - change the structure, and you change the state.

How do you think about your good and not-so-good performances? Realise that *how* you're thinking may very well be holding you back. Deliberately *choose* the type of words and pictures that are going to build those positive states I listed earlier.

Environment. Environment consists of all the *other things* around you that can influence your state. It encompasses both the *social* and *physical* environment, and includes the weather conditions; the venue; your coach and team mates; the officials; your opponents; the audience; your equipment; and so on.

Environment encompasses both the *social* and *physical* aspects of your environs.

To give an example of how environment can affect performance, imagine competing in a place and it's a cold wet day, the venue is dirty and littered with papers, the equipment is old and poorly maintained, the officials disorganised and inefficient, your team mates slovenly and disinterested, and there's half a dozen bored looking spectators barracking for the opposition. Maybe you've even experienced times like that!

Compare that situation to another day where its warm and sunny with a light breeze blowing, the venue is clean and fresh looking, all the equipment is new and well maintained, everything is run like clockwork by the officials, your team mates are sharp and dressed smartly, and there is a huge crowd of your supporters buzzing with excitement. It makes a difference doesn't it?

Another example of how environment can affect your state is given by the person who is playing really well ... until they notice one of their relatives, or close friends, or someone they really want to impress, in the audience .... then their game falls apart!

I think it's important to also recognise that, while environment can affect your state, *it does so only in as much as you allow it to affect the other two - your physiology and ideology.*

128

The environment only affects your state by its influence on your posture and your thinking - and by attending to building positive states using strong physiology and a positive ideology, you can maintain peak performance states *regardless of the environment.*

Having said this, I think it imperative to point out that the effect of the environment is often very subtle and unconscious, and so giving some attention to building a positive environment for peak performance is a good way to encourage positive states - particularly in those people who have not yet developed the ability to consistently *self-manage* their own emotional states.

Two simple things you can do, both individually and collectively, is to ensure that your working and sporting environments are uplifting and inspiring. I've been to too many sports clubs where the clubroom is filthy, there is a layer of dust over everything, the equipment is poorly maintained, and the club office bearers are not the most organised and motivated of individuals! This just isn't good enough. If your club is aiming to win the championship, you want to start with your club rooms - make them look like a champion's club rooms!

The environment affects your state only in as much as you allow it to affect your physiology and ideology.

Follow the same advice personally - make up a 'victory wall' of your successes and achievements and have some motivational posters around your office or room. I also suggested to North Sydney Rugby League Club when consulting for them, to have videos of players scoring trys, making important tackles, and so on. You could do the same. *Success is a result of the little things that help you and your team feel valued and important.*

TRIGGERS

For excellence in performance, I've found that there are two specific states that are particularly useful for sportspeople to develop and use regularly: what I call *uptime* and *downtime*. Uptime is a state of total *external* sensory focus and awareness, without any internal thoughts, images or feelings. Downtime is a state of total *internal* sensory focus and awareness, without any distractions from external sensory input.

Remember - success is a result of the little things that make you and your team feel valued and important.

It's been found that the top sportspeople have well developed skills in both these areas. Uptime states are useful for when actually playing - because you play best when your external sensory input and automatic reactions are not distracted by internal thoughts and imaginings. Most sportspeople who have had those peak experiences in their sport where they have experienced being in the 'zone' will tell you that they weren't thinking *anything* - they just experienced their body playing totally naturally and unconsciously.

Downtime states, on the other hand, are important for developing motivation, in setting goals, in visualising particular plays or movements prior to execution, and for reviewing past performances.

In order to achieve anything, we first want to 'see' it into being - this process can be encouraged through the use of visualisation techniques, but in order to visualise effectively, we want to be in a downtime state.

So an important skill all sportspeople want to develop is the ability to *switch states*, to utilise the most appropriate state for their best performance in any given situation. Of course, uptime and downtime states are just as important in public speaking, sales, negotiations, and other work contexts too.

An important skill you will want to develop, is the ability to utilise both uptime and downtime states.

You want to be able to call up your internal feelings of strong self motivation and desire to win if you're down two sets to love and match point against you. And you want to be able to reflect on a performance objectively and evaluate it non-judgementally, to work out how to improve after a poor performance. And you want to be able to get totally in the 'zone' where you can allow your body to just 'play', without distracting thoughts or self doubts interfering, when you're actually competing.

The best way to develop this *personal facility of control* over your own state is through the use of *sensory triggers*. A sensory trigger is simply a physical stimulus that you train your body to associate with a particular state, and which you can then use to 'switch on' that state in yourself as required, by using the trigger. It's what is known as 'stimulus - response conditioning', and it works in the same way as a light switch. You train your neurology to *automatically respond* in a precise, positive way to a specific stimulus - in the same way that flicking the light switch turns on the electric light.

One way to develop a *personal facility of control* over your own state is building and using *sensory triggers*.

Triggers are common in human experience - the trouble is, that most people have built *negative* triggers for themselves, rather than positive ones. Some common examples of triggers which affect our state are: phobic responses such as fainting at the sight of blood, or freaking out on seeing a spider; and also common emotional *reactions* such as feeling threatened by a particular facial expression or tone of voice; a certain smell 'triggering' a vivid past memory; hearing a particular song on the radio which reminds you of a past relationship; or getting 'stage-fright' in front of an audience.

Triggers are common, but most people have made *negative* triggers, rather than *positive* ones.

Common examples of triggers in sport are the automatic response to stop play when the umpire whistles; anxiety prior to a big match; or getting angry at a dubious line call. The Maori Haka that the All Blacks use prior to a rugby match is a great example of a trigger for building very powerful team spirit and aggressive states in the players; and being on the verge of losing is often a trigger for top players to switch up a gear.

If you've read the *Sportsmind* book, or listened to any of the *Sportsmind* tapes, you will have experienced how to build and use a relaxation, or downtime, trigger for yourself. Downtime triggers like this are excellent for those people who experience over-anxiousness, and need to relax. However, some players are just the opposite - they're *too* relaxed, and they need to 'switch on' and be more aggressive and hungry to win. Sportspeople like this benefit from building an 'uptime' trigger, and using it regularly to deliberately create more positive, focused states in themselves before, and during, competition.

Fortunately, you don't have to engage in the Haka to get into a positive performance state! Can you imagine the ladies at the grand final of the bowls tournament doing the Haka to get into the performance 'zone'!

Uptime triggers are usually simple physical stimuli - such as clenching your left hand strongly, or saying a particular power word, or visualising a specific power symbol to yourself - which you use as needed to generate the positive state you want.

> **You don't have to engage in the Haka to get into a positive performance state!**

You can have lots of different triggers for different positive states, and I've generally found that after using them for a while, they become automatic, and you will only need to use them if for some reason you lose your concentration or confidence.

One good idea is to associate your positive states to something that is *always* in your performance environment. For example, when I give public talks I like to have a lectern - not because I use it all that much, but because it's a *trigger* for me. If I feel I'm not reaching the audience, or I forget my talk, I simply walk over to the lectern and get back into a positive state. Likewise, you can have some item of equipment - a glove, a racquet, a pair of shoes, etc. as your positive trigger. One basketballer I know, uses the smell of the basketball to switch himself on!

Of course, be aware that if you depend *too* much on *external* triggers, you can lose confidence if that special thing is not there! So I encourage you to first build strong *self-based* triggers for the kinds of state you want to exhibit.

BUILDING A POSITIVE PERFORMANCE TRIGGER : THE *CIRCLE OF EXCELLENCE*

Problems occur for people when they confuse internal and external states, and they are not clearly in one or the other. For instance, have you ever tried to concentrate on some study or a work project, or do a relaxation and visualisation exercise, and been distracted by *external* sounds, or feelings? Or, have you ever been plagued by an *internal* critical voice or negative imagination when actually playing a match, or giving a talk, and had your performance suffer as a consequence?

Improve your performance by having powerful triggers for both internal and external states.

The key to more consistent performance is to be aware of the difference between the need for uptime, (or external focus) states; and downtime (or internal focus) states, and to have clear, powerful triggers for both of these states to call upon at will. The way to build such powerful triggers for yourself, is to simply *practice* associating the state with the trigger, until it becomes an automatic response you can elicit at will.

Triggers are established by *practice* - associating the state with the trigger, until it becomes automatic.

The best *self-based* trigger I know of, is what is called the *Circle of Excellence* technique, and I discuss how to do this for yourself in the following exercise, in which you're going to develop a powerful positive resource state and trigger.

I've outlined two other simple exercises for building uptime and downtime triggers in the *Sportsmind* book, and if you've listened to some of the *Sportsmind* tapes, then you will also have had some practice in building a strong *downtime* state for yourself, and associating that state to the trigger of holding your fingers together. The purpose of the following exercise is to associate a powerful uptime resource state to a different, easy-to-use trigger : clenching your *non-dominant hand.*

Use clenching your non-dominant hand as the trigger for your powerful performance state.

I suggest using the non-dominant hand as your trigger for two reasons: Firstly, many sportspeople are holding a racquet, bat, club, or whatever in their dominant hand, and you may want to use the trigger when actually playing. Secondly, you want the trigger to work *unconsciously* and *automatically*, and of course our non-dominant hand is more in touch with the unconscious than the dominant hand.

This exercise is called building a *'Circle of Excellence'*, and like many of the other exercises in this book has been adapted from Terry McClendon's NLP Practitioner Training Course.

Basically the idea is to create an imaginary circle on the floor, about two to three meters in diameter, (I usually draw a real circle in chalk on the floor when I do this exercise with clients), and then build into that circle positive memories one at a time, to which you also associate the clenching of your non-dominant hand. Obviously the more positive memories you can build in to the circle the better, but for the purposes of this exercise, you're going to use *six* positive memories.

Once you've built the circle, and associated it to the trigger, you then 'pick it up' and store it in your mind; then before you hit the drive, or serve the tennis ball, or give the speech, or take the penalty shot at goal, or stand at the blocks, or make the presentation to the boss, or whatever you do in your sport or work situations - you put that circle of excellence down, and step into it as you 'fire' your trigger. Then go and perform superbly.

If you do this properly, what happens is that *it recodes the same neural pathways that led to success in those previous positive memories*, and so allows you to do so *again* - automatically, and without having to 'think about it' or 'try hard' to do so, because it works at a *neuro-muscular*, or physiological level, *not* at the level of conscious thought. It creates what is known as a 'muscle memory'.

> **The circle of excellence builds a positive 'muscle memory' by refiring the same neural pathways that led to success in those previous positive memories.**

Let me explain what I mean by this. As I have mentioned before, any behaviour, whether it be lifting your arm, hitting a golf ball straight down the fairway, or getting nervous before an exam, can be understood to be a consequence of a specific mental program, or a specific set of neurological 'circuits' which fire in the brain. Everything we do out in the external world, every action, every feeling and every performance is a result of something that first happens in our mind at a neurological level.

> **Every performance is a result of processes that first happen in our mind at a neurological level.**

This technique works at this neurological level by associating a specific trigger to the neural 'programs' that led to previous excellent performance behaviours and positive states, and because it works at this neural level it's extremely powerful and effective.

Of course the key to making it work is to be very, very clear in choosing the positive resource states you want, and in building them in yourself. Take your time and fully recover all the sensory details of the success experiences you are going to associate to the trigger, so that you lock in the exact neural pathway for the positive state.

Making the exercise work by fully recovering all the sensory details of the success experiences you're going to associate to the trigger.

Do recognise also that the specific positive memories and states that you choose to build into your circle and associate with the trigger, don't necessarily have to come from the exact same contexts. For instance, I worked with a golfer once who had lost confidence with his short irons, and one of the positive memories which he used to build confidence into his circle of excellence was from a *work* context.

What is important is to make sure that you fully recover the memory from an *associated* or *in body* perspective, and that you re-experience as fully as you can *all* the sensory details of that past performance. That is, you *see* what you saw from *in your body* back then; you *hear* what you heard back then; you *feel* again the movements of your body, and what you felt emotionally then; and you even *smell* the smells around you again, if there were smells associated with that place.

It's also useful to recognise that you can build a circle of excellence in a couple of different ways. For instance, you can build a circle of excellence for a specific *aspect* of your game that you want to improve; or you can build a circle which works on overall positive performance and confidence.

So a golfer might like to build a specific circle of excellence for their putting, or their bunker shots; or on the other hand build a circle of excellence for the overall performance and positive feeling states they would like to have when playing. Likewise a tennis player might establish a circle of excellence for their serve, or maybe their backhand volley; or on the other hand, to recapture the general positive *feeling states* experienced in top past performances.

You can build a circle for a specific *aspect* of your game, or for overall positive performance/confidence.

For this reason, this particular technique is exceptionally useful for helping athletes, (or sales staff), who are currently experiencing a slump in form - because it helps to recapture the positive feeling states from the past and make them available *again* through the use of the positive trigger.

Before you begin the exercise, it's helpful if you stop for a few minutes to think about some past top performances and positive states that you have experienced. Make a list of half a dozen performances that you can recall clearly, that were highs for you and that you would like to build into your circle of excellence now. You might also like to find a piece of chalk, and draw a 2 to 3 meter circle on the floor, to help you visualise your circle. Do this now.

EXERCISE : Building a Circle of Excellence

1. Create your circle. Now standing *outside* of the circle, think of a time when you performed particularly well in your sport, and see that time in the circle, as if you were watching a movie of it. Notice when it was, where you were, other people, etc. .... Now step back into that time (step *into* the circle) and relive all the sensory details of it. What you saw, heard, and especially what you felt. Intensify the feelings, and as you feel them peak, clench your non-dominant hand, and say a trigger word or phrase to yourself. Leave the experience there, and step out of the circle

2. Repeat the above steps for another five or more positive experiences or feelings, programming them into your circle *one at a time*, following the same procedure.

3. Futurepace to upcoming event. From outside the circle, think of an important future event at which you'd like to have all those positive skills and feelings. See that time in the circle, now as you step into that future time (step *into* the circle), fire your trigger (squeeze hand and say trigger word or phrase), and pre-live a top performance. Experience all the sensory details - seeing, hearing and feeling your excellent performance from inside your body in that *future time*.

4. Pick up your circle of excellence, and store it in your mind. The next time you're about to step up to the tee, or onto the court or playing field, or wherever you perform in your sport or work, take a few moments to imagine your circle, step into it and fire your triggers, and feel again those positive emotional states ..... then go out and perform at your best.

CASE STUDIES :   Golf, Cricket, Tennis, Shooting, and Triathlon

This circle of excellence technique is a very powerful tool. I spent *just twenty minutes* taking a golfer who was experiencing the putting 'yips', (ie. a loss of confidence at putting, resulting in even very short putts being missed), through the exercise, and a week later I received a letter in the mail which consisted of a yellow piece of paper on which was drawn a green circle. In the centre of the circle was a newspaper clipping showing their name as having won the local club competition!

I should also note that up until that time this person had never won a single club competition! It works!

> **Up until doing the Circle of Excellence exercise she had never won a single club competition!**

The technique is particularly useful for golf, because of the nature of the game - where for a few seconds you want to be totally focused and positive, and then you walk for five minutes to your ball again. For the same reason, it's also excellent for cricket, bowls, shooting, and similar 'stop - start' sports.

Consequently, I've worked with lots of golfers with the technique, but the best result of anyone I've worked with, was from a cricketer, who prior to attendance at a *Sportsmind Concentration* workshop, (which includes this *Circle of Excellence* exercise), had a batting average of just 16.

> **After doing the Circle of Excellence she scored 132 not out, and 98, in her next two innings.**

In the week following completion of the workshop she subsequently scored 132 not out, and 98, in her next two innings, and finished the season with a batting average of 90! She also wrote after attending another of my workshops, on *Visualisation*: *"I made another 98! I also made my first stumping in cricket as wicket keeper - I visualised before every game how I'd do it!"*

Another sportsperson who had excellent results using this exercise, is a tennis player who was having difficulty with loss of confidence, and in particular finishing off matches. She would win the first set and have a lead in the second, only to eventually lose the match in three sets. Following some work with her using both this technique, (and another technique called *'Limitations to Excellence'*), she won a big tournament, and jumped 100 places in her international ranking - to her career best!

She won a big tournament, and jumped 100 places in her international ranking after the exercise!

I've also had good success with the technique with both a pistol shooter and shotgun shooter, both of whom were able to shoot well in practice, but intense nervousness caused them to shoot poorly in competition, particularly in shoot-out situations. This exercise gave them an easy-to-use trigger to overcome this.

The final example is of a Triathlete who came to me for lack of confidence in his sport, allowing himself to feel intimidated by other athletes and peers, even though he was just as good and equally as fit. It was this lack of confidence and negative feelings that were holding him back. After doing the exercise, he improved not only his confidence in his triathlon competing, but also at his work.

USING THE CIRCLE OF EXCELLENCE IN PRACTICE

Now it's also useful to recognise that your 'circle' doesn't have to be a 2 meter circle: you might like to imagine your 'area of excellence' to be the tennis court; or judo mat; or playing field; or swimming pool; or even your bicycle!

Of course you can also use this idea for other performance areas: public speaking; important meetings or delicate negotiations; exams; sales situations; and so on. I use my trigger whenever I have to give a really important talk, and when I do, I automatically step into a state of confidence and positive performance, and I always speak well. So do use it elsewhere in your life as well: sales people might like to have their area of excellence around the telephone; if you're a student or writer, your circle of excellence might be your desk, or word processor; musicians can have their instrument as their trigger for excellence.

Your 'circle' doesn't have to be a 2 meter circle - it might be your desk, or bicycle, or telephone!

Of course, after a short while, you no longer have to deliberately use your trigger - it becomes something automatic and natural, and you always perform well without having to try hard.

One final hint to make this work in your sport or at work even more quickly is to deliberately use your trigger *consciously* to build in good shots, strokes, and performances *at the time they happen*. If you do an excellent drive, or an unplayable ace, or give an excellent presentation or talk .... stop immediately after, and clench your non-dominant hand, and deliberately intensify the good feeling of it to imprint it into your neurology.

Likewise, if you do a poor shot, or have an off day, take a moment to deliberately *walk away* from the area and *dissociate from that performance* .... imagine yourself 'throwing it away', and then go back to your performance area, and re-play in your mind exactly how you wanted to have done the shot, given the presentation, or performed.

Use your trigger *consciously* to build in good shots, strokes, and performances *at the time they happen.*

Doing this trains your neurology to automatically and consistently focus on and move toward positive states and performances, and to move away from the negative. If you've ever watched any top cricketers or golfers, they often go through this process. If a cricketer does a bad shot, you will often see them walk away from the stumps, then come back and replay how they wanted to have hit the ball. If you do this, it allows you to not contaminate the area where you want to perform at your best with negative states or performances.

Likewise, replaying good shots or strokes and reliving previous good performances is a very simple yet very powerful tool. Get into the habit of doing it. [This is of course, the ARIA and ALIA techniques I discussed in Chapter 1 of *Sportsmind*]

Of course, there is one important pre-requisite for all these processes to work ... and that is you want to have a *commitment to excellence* in your sport - and in your life. Do you? Are you committed to personal excellence?

Do you have a *commitment to excellence* in your life?

FROM LIMITATIONS TO EXCELLENCE

I mentioned earlier that you want to make negative feelings a call to change yourself, or the situation, in some way - *to use negative states as triggers to go for your resources.*

So next time you start to feel angry, or depressed, or unmotivated, or whatever negative feeling plagues you - *let it become a trigger to ask yourself the question,* "What would I *rather* be feeling?". Then deliberately take action to build a more positive state in yourself.

> **Use negative states as triggers to go for your positive resources.**

Of course, as I pointed out earlier, an essential prerequisite for this to work is for you to be *aware* of your feelings - and more particularly, to develop a *very refined sense of your feelings* so you can recognise the very first tendrils of a negative emotion, so you can nip them in the bud.

> **There is a window of opportunity for you to change a negative feeling, before it takes 'hold'.**

Most feelings tend to build up from subtle beginnings to full blown emotions over a period of time. Of course, the length of time varies from person to person and from context to context, but the point is that *there is usually a window of opportunity for you to change a negative feeling, before it takes 'hold'.*

Too often people have only a very gross feeling sense, and they only notice they're feeling bad when they're fully into it. As a consequence, they get stuck in the negative feelings - because feelings also take time to diminish. Once you really get into a feeling - whether it be positive or negative - it takes a while to come down, doesn't it?

Consequently, an extremely useful exercise to do is to set up 'circuit breakers' for negative feelings and emotions - the purpose of which is to immediately back out of the negative feeling, and go instead for a positive resource state. As soon as you feel the very first indication that you're getting into a non-resourceful feeling, you can immediately change it.

Set up unconscious, negative feeling circuit breakers with the 'Limitations to Excellence' exercise.

You can do this process *consciously* - that is, as soon as you notice yourself getting into a negative state, you can change your physiology, ideology or environment in some way to get into a more positive feeling. However, there is often a very strong existing trigger for the negative emotion already established, and it's become an ingrained habit. The person gets into the negative feeling very quickly, and they don't have time to slow the process down for such a conscious approach. Phobic responses are examples of this - as soon as they see or hear the trigger, WHAM!, they're straight into an intense feeling response!

So it's even better if you can learn to do this process *unconsciously*, by setting up an unconscious negative feeling circuit breaker by using the following 'Limitations to Excellence' exercise.

EXERCISE : Limitations to Excellence

1. Establish two 'circles' - one a 'limiting' circle and one an 'excellence' circle. Draw them about 3 - 4 meters apart.

2. Pick a negative emotion that you want to work with, and in the same way as you did previously for the circle of excellence exercise, build in memories of experiencing this negative emotion - but DO NOT build a trigger for it. Also establish your circle of excellence, and add in any further positive experiences or states that might be useful to you here.

3. Step into and out of each circle, experiencing the states. Now from a neutral observer position, compare and contrast the visual, auditory, and kinaesthetic details of each state.

4. Again from the neutral position, begin to approach the limiting circle until you become aware of the first 'sign' of getting into the negative feeling. Immediately step back, turn and go directly into your circle of excellence, and recover the positive feelings using your positive trigger, (squeeze hand).

5. Repeat step 4, *five times*. Now from the neutral position, identify the *positive intention* of negative state, and integrate that positive intention into yourself.

6. Futurepace the new response to the old trigger. Think of an upcoming event or situation in the future which *had the potential* for you to react with the negative feeling - something with the old trigger in it. Picture and hear that situation, and as you do, step into your circle of excellence and fire your positive trigger. Feel the good feelings, and for a few minutes pre-play your new positive response in this future context.

You will note that this technique builds on the 'Circle of Excellence' exercise you completed earlier, (you use the circle of excellence you made for yourself again in this exercise), so do ensure you've completed it properly before doing this exercise. Of course, you may choose to build a totally new positive circle, containing other positive experiences and emotions - and this may in fact be necessary if your current circle doesn't contain the kind of positive emotions and experiences appropriate to the negative one you want to change.

It may be necessary to build a totally new positive circle, with other positive experiences and emotions.

Also, you will notice that I stress that you don't build a trigger for the negative circle, while you definitely do for the positive circle. Why would you want to have a trigger for a negative state?

It's very important to understand the difference between the observer position, and being in either of the circles. The observer position is a place *outside of the influence of either circle*, and from which you can, in a neutral state, simply observe - without feeling, or getting involved in that state - what you experience in each circle. On the other hand, when you're actually in each circle, you totally involve yourself in reliving the experience, and feeling the feelings, either positive or negative.

Do ensure that you maintain the distinctions between each of the three positions - observer, excellence, and limitation, because if you 'contaminate' any of the positions with feelings from another, the exercise won't work as effectively. It's helpful to 'shake off' the feelings in each circle, leaving them there, before stepping back out to the observer position.

What really makes this exercise work as a circuit breaker is step 4. It's vitally important here to step back out of the negative state at the first 'sign' of the negative feeling - don't let yourself get into the negative state. Stop, step back from it, and immediately go for your positive resource state and fully access it. Repeating this step over and over is what establishes the circuit breaker.

Essentially you're teaching your brain to sensitise itself to negative feelings. As soon as you start to feel 'bad', you immediately and unconsciously look for positive resource states, and go for them!

You teach your brain to immediately look for positive resource states, as soon as you start to feel 'bad'.

Some people take *so long* to get out of negative states! Why wait? Why not feel good *now*? Think about it - if you're depressed, or anxious, or lonely, or angry, or whatever negative emotion, it's not going to last forever, is it? There will be a time when that feeling will change - be it in an hour, tomorrow, next week or five years from now! No one - unless they're psychotic - stays in any one feeling state for extended periods of time; it's not natural to do so. Things change around us, and part of being alive is responding to those changing circumstances, with our thoughts and feelings.

So if it's a fact that you *will feel differently* about this situation at some time in the future, why wait? Why not feel good now? You've learned the 'lesson' from the experience, so why continue to feel bad? It's pointless, and worse, it 's counterproductive!

Why wait? Why not feel good *right now*?

In step 5 I mentioned identifying the *positive intention* behind the negative state, and then integrating this positive intention into yourself. This is an 'ecology' step - ensuring that the change you make is in harmony with all aspects of yourself.

Realise that you're experiencing the negative emotion for *some reason* - there is a positive intention behind it. Perhaps you're angry because someone has taken advantage of you, and the positive intention is to stick up for yourself more. Perhaps you're lonely because you don't know how to talk to people, and the positive intention is to get you to learn to get on with other people. Perhaps you're feeling unmotivated because you're in a job you hate, or you're training too hard, and the positive intention is to find a career that inspires you, or to take a break.

> **There is a reason for every negative emotion - there is some *positive intention* underlying it.**

You worked with positive intentions in the ecology step of the SMARTER goal achieving process, likewise by acknowledging the intention here, you encourage more successful change.

The final step is to 'futurepace' the new response to the old trigger. I also used this term in the *Circle of Excellence* exercise, and 'futurepacing' is an important NLP process that you will see included time and again in exercises. Futurepacing sets up a positive future visualisation of the desired outcome, pre-programming your neurology to respond that way in a future context, in which you probably would have reacted negatively. It also acts as a checking system - if you can't do the futurepace properly, if you can't see/feel yourself acting in a positive state - then something went wrong in the previous parts of the exercise.

'STUCK' STATES

In addition to building circuit breakers for negative states by using the previous exercise, you can also teach yourself, or others, how to quickly get out of negative or limiting states. Sometimes people get themselves into a negative state - be it anger, unconfidence, depression, apathy, or whatever - and get 'stuck' there. The following exercise offers a way of 'loosening up' your state changing muscles.

An *anchor* is a term used to describe the sophisticated stimulus-response conditioning process used in NLP.

It's a particularly useful exercise, because like both the previous exercises, it teaches you how to take charge of your own emotional states through the use of *self anchors*, or triggers. An *anchor* is a term used in NLP to describe the sophisticated stimulus-response conditioning process used to link emotional states, or other behaviours, to visual, auditory or kinaesthetic cues. We've used primarily kinaesthetic anchors, (squeezing your hand), as they are easy to understand and usually the most effective, but certainly NLP practitioners also make use of auditory and visual anchors as well.

EXERCISE : Getting Out of a 'Stuck' State

1. **Establish a strong positive resource state and anchor it.**
2. **Go to a neutral state, and then test your anchor.**
3. **Get yourself into negative 'stuck' state. Amplify it until you're really feeling that negative feeling strongly.**
4. **Get yourself out of it, by 'firing' the resource state anchor.**

AMPLIFYING POSITIVE STATES

Finally, in addition to working with negative states, you can also *amplify your positive states* - turn your good feelings into fantastic feelings! The way to do this is to work with the submodalities of the positive emotional states, and crank them up.

I've explained how changing the size, brightness, closeness, etc. of the visual elements, or changing the tone, volume, tempo, etc. of the auditory elements, of a state can increase or decrease the intensity of your feelings. But you can also work with the *kinaesthetic submodalities* directly to amplify it.

Increase or decrease the intensity of your feelings by changing the *kinaesthetic submodalities* of the state.

For example, most feelings have movement of some kind, and the movements have to start in some place and finish in another place. These movements also have a certain speed and tempo, an intensity, and an extent - how far they extend. If you link the end of the feeling back to the beginning, increase the tempo and intensity, and then have the feelings double or triple their extension, you can greatly enhance the positive state! Try it for yourself now. Pick a good feeling - say motivation or confidence - and do the above, and feel what happens!

Finally, I think the key to mastering your state is to firstly notice what your *habitual feelings* are, and then set up unconscious circuit breakers for the negative states, and amplifiers for the positive states. It's not what you feel *occasionally* that affects you, but rather your habitual feelings. Make sure you choose *champion feelings* to make your habits!

"You are a champion because you are positive — recognising that nothing good ever comes from negativity."

CHAPTER 6 :

CHAMPION
THOUGHTS

THE MENTAL EDGE

Your performance is profoundly influenced by your thoughts - by the things you imagine and say to yourself.

Thoughts are powerful - thoughts *make* things happen. Thoughts are the building blocks from which you create your beliefs, attitudes, behaviours, and every aspect of your performance at work, or in sport. *Every* thought affects you in some way - either empowering you, or limiting you. There are no 'neutral' thoughts.

Yet few people recognise the enormous power of their moment to moment thinking, and fewer still actually use this awareness in their daily life.

Champions give themselves a *mental edge* by standing guard at the door of their mind - by taking control of their thinking, and by deliberately choosing to focus on the positive.

MASTERING YOUR MIND

Everyone knows they're supposed to 'be positive' - to think positively, and to discourage negativity. Yet for so many people thoughts just seem to 'happen' before they know about it! People tell me all the time, "I can't help it. I just automatically do it!"

Thoughts don't 'just happen' - *you think them*!

At which point I tell them that's a cop out, and a load of rubbish. Thoughts don't 'just happen' to you - *you think them*! There can be no escaping the fact that *you choose your thoughts* - how else could they get there?

Yet even knowing this, some people still indulge in negative thinking, and problem focus - rather than looking for solutions and always expecting the best for yourself.

Look for solutions and expect the best for yourself.

Part of the problem is, of course, that negative thinking has become a habit - not only for individuals, but for the society in general. Like any habit, it takes effort and *willingness to change*. So the issue for many people is to be *personally convinced* of the detriment of negative thinking on their performance and in their lives, and of the enormous advantages that accrue to those who continually focus on positive, possibility thoughts.

Let me give you an example to convince you, and hopefully encourage your willingness to let go of the habit!

CASE STUDY : Karrie Webb and the 1998 Australian Ladies Masters.

It was rather appropriate, and certainly serendipitous, that on the afternoon I sat down to begin this chapter, Karrie Webb was walking down the eighteenth hole to the applause of thousands of supporters to claim her first Australian title, winning by five strokes, and having set a course record the day before.

She began the final round with a lead of five shots, but sports commentators were at pains to point out that in the same event just the year before, she 'squandered' an identical lead and lost by a stroke. All through the morning, the question was: would she falter again? It certainly looked ominous when her nearest rival cut her lead down to three, and then to only two shots. However a wonderful second shot and a superb 18 meter putt saw her capture an eagle on the 15th hole, reclaiming a four shot lead, and eventual victory by five shots.

I was listening to her interviewed after the match, and was pleased to hear her say, in response to a question about whether she was worried about repeating last year's stumble, that she "didn't think about being only one shot or two shots ahead", she "thought about wanting to score 2 under or 3 under par". "I kept focusing on *my* game", she said.

She succeeded by focusing on her *own performance*, her own game, rather than on her opponents.

In contrast to the previous year, (when she had focused on her lead), when she focused on her desired performance, the results were achieved. This is exactly what I have spoken about before - the importance of the *focus* of your thinking.

TAKING CONTROL OF YOUR THOUGHTS

Every performance, be it in sport, at work, in an exam for school, in public speaking, or wherever, starts *in your mind*. The best performances occur when you take control of your performance by taking control of your thinking. All control begins by taking control of the thoughts you think.

All control begins by taking control of your thoughts.

But what does it mean to 'take control of your thinking', and *how* do you do it - particularly if you're someone who's been habitually negative?

I've heard people say to me, and others, time and time again, 'you've got to be more *positive*, you want to think *positively*'. I've heard coaches tell players, and sales managers tell their staff, to be more 'focused', or 'determined', or 'positive', or 'hungry to win', or 'confident'. But these words don't really say anything, do they? They're just words - and they don't tell you *how* to be more positive, focused, confident, or whatever.

One of the beauties of NLP, in stark contrast to other cognitive psychologies, is it's insistence on detailed *process descriptions* for behaviours, rather than just theories, concepts, or platitudes. A process description tells you precisely *what to do, and how to do it*. It's a bit like a cooking recipe: follow the directions properly, and you'll end up with the result you want - be it a chocolate sponge cake, a vegetarian lasagne, or a positive mental attitude!

So what is the process description for attaining a positive mental attitude - how do you build it; what do you *do*?

THE FOUR CONTROL KEYS

I've identified four 'control keys' for mastering your mind: Awareness, Focus, Meaning, and Timing. All of these control keys depend on the master key of *decisions*, which I discussed in an earlier chapter. Remember, everything begins with a *decision*. So make the decision now to take control of your mind, and then I'll show you how to implement it.

Control of your mind begins with a *decision* to do so.

Let's look at and discuss each of the four control keys in turn, so you can feel confident putting each of them into practice within yourself.

1. AWARENESS

The first is to accept the simple awareness that there exists a place within you, a point if you will, at which or in which, thoughts come into existence. It could be described as a space, or a moment of decision, within which you *choose a particular thought over another.* Such a place, or process, *must exist* - for there must be some way whereby you choose which thought to go with at any instant of time.

I call this place, the *choice point of thought.*

Once you accept the existence of this choice point of thought - the first key is to find and become familiar with it within you, and through practice, take control of it.

There is a place within you where thoughts arise.

EXERCISE : Connecting With the 'Choice Point of Thought'

The easiest way to become familiar with this choice point of thought, is to simply sit quietly, turn your eyes slightly upwards as if you were looking at something a meter or so above your head, and become aware of the top of your head.

Now deliberately move your attention, or awareness, to the top of your head.

When you do this, you experience a greater sense of control over your thinking process, almost as if you were *above your thoughts*. In fact you will notice a quietening of your thoughts, and an inner clarity or perceptiveness that perhaps you've never experienced before.

Take a few minutes, right now, and do this. Just sit with it - stay with your attention in this place for as long as you can. This will probably only be a few minutes at first, but with practice you will be able to 'switch' to this position at will.

It's also a useful exercise to regularly 'check in' throughout the day, and attend to where your awareness currently is. For instance, where is your awareness of yourself, right now? In what part of your body do you experience your sense of self? Is it in your body, if so, what part of your body? Do you experience yourself in your head, if so where in your head? Do you experience yourself slightly out of or behind your body, if so, where exactly - how far back, or up?

Take a few minutes to familiarise yourself with your 'normal' and most common 'perceptual position'.

I use the term 'perceptual position' to identify the fact that how you experience the world, *including how you experience yourself* - is just *one* way of looking at it, or you! There are other perceptual positions, some of which may be of significant advantage to you - in both your work, and in your sport.

When asked, "Where do you experience your sense of self?", many people generally point to their head - and I would have to say that this is where I most commonly experience my 'self' as well - generally right behind my eyes.

The position of your awareness is simply a *choice*.

Through my study of NLP and also Aikido, I've learned that the position of your awareness is however, like all other behaviours, simply a choice. I've learned to *move my awareness* - to become more aware of my body, and in particular to take my awareness from my head, and move it to my centre when I do Aikido.

However I think it's important to recognise that *no one perceptual position is necessarily any 'better' than another.* Having your awareness in your centre is great for physical activities involving balance and coordination, such as Aikido or other sports, but it's probably not all that useful for doing a maths exam! Likewise, the perceptual position I've called the 'choice point of thought' is excellent for quieting your mind and giving you a strong sense of self control and self direction - but it's probably not all that useful for enjoying the pleasures of the flesh, such as a massage, or a cuddle with your partner!

No perceptual position is any 'better' than another.

FIRST, SECOND, AND THIRD POSITIONS

What is important, I believe, *is the ability to switch perceptual positions at will* - to choose and make use of the most appropriate perceptual position for the task at hand. In the same way that you can choose your emotional state, *you also have control over your perceptual position.* The trouble is that most people just experience one perceptual position, and so severely limit their learning and performance potential.

> **It's important to be able to switch perceptual positions at will.**

There are three general perceptual positions: first position, second position, and third position, and they correspond roughly to the literary terms first person, second person and third person: when I'm in first position I am myself, I speak *as myself*; in second position I experience and empathise *with others*; and in third position I take a neutral or observer view, and I speak *about myself or others.* Also, within each position there are further 'sub-positions' or variations.

First position is that of very much experiencing yourself in your body - seeing, hearing, feeling, smelling, and tasting all sensory experiences directly. As I mentioned above, within this first position you may also choose to place your attention in different parts of your body, and vary your perceptions accordingly. This position is also called an *associated* position, because you are fully associated to all your sensory experiences.

In first position you are fully associated to your senses.

Second position is the act of empathising with another; of 'stepping into their shoes', and experiencing yourself and the world, from their perspective, thoughts, and feelings. Again, in this second position there can be variation in the position : you may choose to associate to their feelings, or to how they see things, or perhaps to their thoughts and opinions.

In second position you associate to another person, animal, or thing.

I think it's also important to note that such an association can also be made to animals, plants, or even 'inanimate' objects or places.

Third position is a *dissociated* perceptual position in which you experience the world from a reference point outside yourself, or another. Seeing yourself from a 'bird's eye view' would be an example of a dissociated position, as would looking at yourself from say two or three meters behind you, or watching yourself on a movie screen, or video. In third position you don't experience your senses directly, but rather you think or feel *about* them.

Third position is a *dissociated* position in which you experience the world from 'out of your body'.

Do recognise that each perceptual position has its advantages - and limitations. For instance, first position is necessary to fully enjoy pleasurable experiences either in real time, or as memories, and also for 'performance' situations such as those experienced in sport or combat, and as I showed in Chapter 4, the ability to associate into a future goal makes it more compelling.

Strong first position perceptions are needed for success in careers such as professional sport; barristers; commodity and futures trading; pilots; truck and taxi drivers; and others who need to be really 'with it' moment to moment.

The limitation of first position is that if you associate to painful or negative experiences or memories, it increases the intensity of your pain, embarrassment, fear, or whatever! Phobias are an example of a negative first position perceptions.

First position is used to enjoy pleasurable experiences.

Second position is obviously necessary to build relationships with people, animals and even 'things'. Sportspeople can use second position to associate to team mates, or even their equipment. You can also associate to a place, or the environment - aboriginal culture, for instance, has a strong second position perception.

Strong second position perceptions are needed for careers such as acting; sales; nursing and medicine; mechanics; receptionists; veterinary science; and environmentalists. Mother Theresa was an individual who personified second position, with her empathy for the poor, and someone such as Jacques Costeau was able to associate to the oceans of the world, and their creatures.

The limitations of second position are that you can become too caught up in 'what other people think or feel', that you deny your own needs and goals.

Second position is used to empathise with others.

Third position is useful for dissociating from negative experiences or memories, such as getting your tooth filled at the dentist, or remembering a car accident or a relationship break up. From third position you can also be 'objective' and see both sides of an argument, so it's also useful in negotiation and teaching.

Third position is used for dissociating from negative experiences or memories.

Strong third position perceptions are needed for careers such as diplomats, judges; scientists; economists; politicians; architects; and writers.

The limitation of third position is the tendency to become cold, unfeeling and calculating. A typical example of a negative extreme of third position perception is the cutting down of native hardwood forests to sell for woodchips for a couple of dollars a tonne, and a few short term jobs!

Interestingly, the study of science is an almost entirely third position pursuit. For instance, to develop his theory of relativity, Einstein did a 'thought experiment' in which he imagined what it would be like to ride on a beam of light - definitely a third position perception! On the other hand, given that science only uses this third position perception in its studies, it only ever really 'understands' about a third of the 'reality' of what it is studying! [This is particularly true of the study of psychology, which tries to understand human *subjectivity* from only an *objective* position!]

What is important is to notice where you *habitually* hold your awareness, and learn to change it at will. Use the following exercises to experiment with different perceptual positions.

EXERCISE : Experiencing First, Second and Third Positions

1. Think of a *positive experience* that involved yourself and at least one other person. For example, it could be a sports performance that you were pleased with; a presentation or speech you've given that you did well; a pleasant evening out with your partner; or something similar.

2. Re-experience the event from *first position*. This means you associate yourself back into your body back then, seeing, hearing, and feeling *exactly* what you saw, heard, and felt back then - from inside your own body. Do this for about five minutes, then bring your attention back to a neutral state.

3. Now go back to the same event, and this time re-experience it from *second position*. This means you associate into someone else in the experience - your opponent, or team mate; a person in the audience; or your partner. Step into *their* body back then, seeing, hearing, and feeling *exactly* what *they* saw, heard, and felt back then. Do this for about five minutes, then bring your attention back to a neutral state.

4. Now go back to the same event, and this time re-experience it from *third position*. View the event from a neutral, outside observer's position. Some positions to use are:
     * from above looking down, (use different heights);
     * from an ant's perspective on the ground looking up;
     * from either side, (use different distances);
     * from behind yourself, looking over your shoulder;
     * from behind the other person.
Do this for about five minutes, then bring your attention back to a neutral state. Conclude the exercise.

Now you would probably have found that one position was easier to get into - it felt more 'natural' to you, while one or perhaps both, of the other perceptual positions were very strange, or you couldn't even experience those positions properly. Perhaps you kept associating when you were supposed to be in the third position; or you kept dissociating when you were supposed to be in the second position!

This is normal - it just shows how much we are all creatures of habit. For this reason it's an excellent learning and awareness exercise - because to extend your performance, you will want to become more familiar with the positions that are *least* comfortable for you.

To improve your performance, you want to become familiar with the *least comfortable* positions.

For example, I find it very easy to be in first, or third positions - while second position is very alien to me! [The one exception to this is 'that when I write I shift from being in first position when writing, then into second position (as an imaginary reader) to check what I've written after every page or so, and then into third position at the end of the chapter to check how it all fits together with the rest of the book.] This is in stark contrast to my wife, who is primarily second position, and finds third position difficult.

I also encourage you to do the above exercise for a *negative* event - perhaps a poor sports performance; or a bad day at work; or an argument with your partner. A word of warning before you do - make sure you've mastered the 'Getting out of a Stuck State' exercise, (see page 150), *before* you go into first position in this exercise!!

CASE STUDY : Tennis Player

How perceptual shifts as I've described can be of significance to sportspeople was demonstrated very clearly to me during the work I did with the tennis player, mentioned in the previous chapter, who was experiencing a lack of ability to finish off games - often losing matches in which she was well ahead. She was also experiencing a lot of self doubt about her abilities, and self consciousness in groups of people.

In both circumstances the problem came from her habitually taking *second position* - ie. associating into what other people are feeling or thinking. For instance she made comments like "I felt sorry for the other player when I 'tubed' her", (a tennis term meaning hitting a winner which leaves your opponent flat footed and looking foolish). Further, to be self conscious, is not really *self* conscious at all, but rather *other* conscious - concerned about what *other* people think of you, or your abilities, or your looks, or your behaviour - a uniquely second position perception.

Through the use of the 'Circle of Excellence' and the other techniques I taught her, she was able to develop an ability to go to first position, particularly in competition, and so overcome her habitual and limiting use of second position.

Top players, when they're playing well, are most often totally in first position - fully in their own body and their own feelings. There's not a lot of benefit in taking second position when you're actually playing, as the above limitations illustrate.

This is not to say that second position is not useful - it is, and particularly so for team sports - however, it's a good idea to identify when and where each perceptual position will get you the outcome you want, and have the ability to switch positions at will.

MODELLING BEHAVIOURS AND QUIETENING THE INTERNAL DIALOGUE

There are two other aspects of awareness that I'd like to outline before moving on to the second key of mental mastery. These are modelling behaviours, and quietening your internal dialogue.

I'm sure you've admired a particular behaviour, skill, or talent of someone else - perhaps their physical skills, or the way they can speak in public or debate an issue, or the way they can quickly gain rapport and communicate effectively one-on-one, or their ability to learn and speak another language, or play a musical instrument.

**Use perceptual shifts to model and emulate
behaviours or talents you would like to have.**

Perceptual shifts can be used to help you model and emulate behaviours or talents you would like to have.

Likewise, it's been identified that one of the keys to peak performance, is to be able to quieten your internal dialogue. When you're in the performance 'zone', your mind is quiet and you're able to focus totally on your external sensory experience, without getting distracted by your talking to yourself. I described this 'uptime' state in the previous chapter, and also included an exercise for building it in the *Sportsmind* book. However, this ability to stop your internal dialogue is often a stumbling block for some people, and there are some other simple 'tricks' you can use to help you quieten your internal dialogue at will.

Use the following exercises to understand and master these skills.

EXERCISE : MODELLING BEHAVIOURS

1. Think of a behaviour, skill or talent that you'd like to have.
2. Think of someone who you admire who has that ability.
3. Go to second position and associate into them: get a feel for how they move, what they see, and what they hear or say to themselves when they're exhibiting that skill or behaviour.
4. Now go to third position (dissociated), and imagine a movie of them exhibiting that skill. Repeat the movie from a number of different views: from above them looking down, from either side, from directly in front, from behind, from ground level, etc. Simply watch and listen to these movies.
5. Still in third position, re-run the movies, only this time put *your face and body* in the movie, doing exactly what they did.
6. Now go to first position and re-run the movie, associating yourself into your body in the movie, feeling the body movements and emotions as you exhibit the skill.
7. Think of a future context in which you'd like to have this skill or behaviour. From third position, see and hear yourself doing so in that future time. Now take first position, and associate to yourself in the future and feel yourself doing it.

EXERCISE : STOPPING INTERNAL DIALOGUE

1. Choose a context where you want to experience internal silence. It may be sitting quietly, walking to work, playing tennis - any context will do.
2. Now attend to all your *external* senses: see, hear, smell, taste and feel outside of you. In particular, tune your eyes to your peripheral vision. See out of the *sides* of your eyes.
3. Press your tongue to your bottom teeth, and hold it there.
4. When you're quiet, you may want to 'lock it in' for future use with a sensory trigger, eg. hold left wrist.

2. FOCUS

The second key to mastering your mind is focus. I've already explained in a previous chapter how your decisions about what you focus upon affects your performance: so you recognise it's important to *focus on what you want* rather than what you want to avoid. Focus on the average, and that's what you'll get. Focus your thinking on the extraordinary individuals, and on the extraordinary in individuals, and amazing things can happen.

Focus your thinking on the extraordinary individuals, and on the extraordinary in individuals.

This is the basis of NLP - modelling the thoughts and feelings of people who excel. Today, too much attention seems to be placed, in my opinion, on the 'average' person - what an average person thinks, what an average person buys, how an average person behaves. To me that's a recipe for mediocrity. Champions excel because they don't focus on the 'average' or the mediocre, but on *doing the things that average people don't do.*

A classic example was Greg Liganus, one of the greatest ever diving champions. I'm sure you remember his 'mistake' in the Olympics where he hit his head on the board - it must have been replayed a hundred times! I heard it reported that when one of the TV stations who had recorded the event for posterity offered to give him a video tape of his mistake, he refused! He knew that if he focused on the mistake, he would reinforce it; he didn't even want to consider the possibility that Greg Liganus could hit his head on the diving board. He knew the secret of focus.

Champions do the things that average people don't.

LIFE CURRENTS

However, there is another aspect of focus that's also important - you want to be aware of 'cross currents' that may be taking you off your intended course.

For instance, let's say you want to swim across a river to reach a point on the other side. Once you're in the river and swimming to the other side, you don't notice the current that's taking you sideways unless you continually refer to your desired destination, and adjust your direction accordingly.

Sometimes it's necessary to allow for the currents in your life, and aim accordingly.

An unaware person, even though they may set themselves a very clearly defined goal or destination, can be swept far off course. So in order to reach your goal, sometimes it's necessary to allow for the currents in our lives, and to deliberately aim to one side of the destination and allow the currents to correct your course, bringing you to exactly where you want to be.

But just what are these 'life currents' that I'm speaking about? Some currents come from external influences, over which we may have very little control, (eg. gravity, weather patterns, state laws, the behaviour of others, etc), and for which we simply want to adjust and adapt accordingly. However there are also currents which are *self generated* by our habitual behaviours and reactions, and these are the most interesting and elusive.

There are also currents which are *self generated*

'FROG SOUP' FOCUS

The best way to describe these self generated currents in your life is to reflect on a simple observation: it's a fact that if you take a frog and put it in a saucepan of cold water, and then gradually heat the water at a rate that is below the level of the frog's ability to detect the temperature change, it will stay there and not jump out - effectively ending up as frog soup! But if you take a frog and throw it directly into hot water, it will immediately jump out and save itself.

**'Frog soup' are areas in our life to which we have
adapted without awareness.**

John Grinder, (one of the developers of NLP), at a seminar I recently attended, likened the areas in our life to which we have simply adapted without awareness, to 'frog soup' situations. These frog soup situations are represented by habits, routines, and repetitive patterns of behaviour that we haven't examined, and simply do without question.

What makes these areas important for consideration is that they are always unconscious until recognised, and similarly exert their 'cross current' influence outside of your awareness. Of course, particularly in successful people, these habits and routines need not necessarily be detrimental, and many certainly exert positive influences. The point is that regardless of whether or not these habits are *currently* leading to success, they may block your ability to become aware of the subtle changes that are below the threshold established by that behavioural pattern, and even though you might be comfortable right now, the water may be heating up, and you not able to notice the temperature rising!

So it's a useful exercise to expand your focus to include these self generated currents in your life. In addition to focusing on your goal, also be aware of the habits and routines you've established, and be willing to do something differently from time to time to provide you with a gauge to test the current water temperature!

What this means in practice is to have strong, positive routines that work for you - and to also vary your 'training' approach every so often to 'catch' or 'stalk' yourself. This enables you to keep improving by consistently stretching yourself.

Vary your training approach every so often to catch, or 'stalk', your habitual patterns.

For instance, my Aikido teacher's usual teaching style follows the pattern of demonstrating and explaining a technique, then the class practices it in pairs. However, every so often he teaches a class in which we get no verbal instructions or explanations - we simply have to watch as it's demonstrated, and then do the technique as best we can. Originally these classes were a real stretch for me, as I found myself very frustrated at not having any verbal explanation, but have recently come to value them as a great opportunity to extend my ability to learn in different ways.

It's been suggested that the art of being good at something is not only knowing what to do or pay attention to, *but also to know what not to do, or pay attention to.* The classic example of this being in rock climbing, where the inexperienced person tenses up whole groups of muscles unnecessarily, and so tires and is unable to complete the climb; while the expert knows to relax all his muscles except those in his fingers, and so conserves energy enabling him to summit out.

172

YOUR 'TRAINING' DIARY

A very useful strategy for identifying these 'frog soup' behaviours in your life is to have a 'training' diary, and to follow your normal behaviours over a period of a couple of weeks, or a month. You might be surprised at the patterns that emerge, and at how 'stuck' you are in certain behaviours.

Of course, when I refer to 'training' here, it doesn't just relate to what you do in your sport, but to all areas of your life. What steps do you follow in order to achieve whatever you do in your work? How do you start the day? What route do you take to work? How do you respond to particular people in your life? What do you do for recreation? What do you eat? What makes you angry? Where can you predict *exactly* how you will behave?

Use the following exercise to broaden your focus to become aware of these 'frog soups' in your life, and begin to do some 'cross training' to break up your habitual patterns and routines :

EXERCISE : TRAINING DIARY

1. Brainstorm for five minutes on a piece of paper to identify the major activities in your life. Eg. sport; work; partner; friends; hobbies; etc.
2. For each area, reflect on what you've done over the past month. What behaviours / routines have been the same?
3. Pick one area to work on this week, and deliberately change your routine. Eg. walk or catch public transport to work instead of driving; change the times or place of your meals; take a different approach in your sports training; act differently to your partner when they get angry; etc.
4. Repeat for the other areas in your life in the coming weeks.

CASE STUDY : Long Distance Runner

The following quote is from a colleague of mine who is a runner, reflecting on the routines he used when competing. Note the importance of his training diary as a resource for confidence building, and also the perceptual shifts that occurred within him just before the race, and his use of a sensory trigger, (the watch), to recapture positive feeling states in other races and contexts!

"While competing as an elite masters athlete in Canada and the USA my preparation before an event consisted of a well rehearsed routine. During the week prior to the event I had established a set program where I tapered my training in the same way each time. Although this was principally to bring me to my physical peak, I always sensed that when I began this countdown in my training, it also acted as a trigger for my mind to begin its preparation.

In particular I would be especially alert to counter the doubts that always seem to be more prevalent during this week. I found it important to put in a lot of effort to maintaining my confidence and positiveness as the event approached.

One method I used was to refer to my training diary and note how well I'd trained in recent weeks, and compare my training to that preceding other events in which I'd performed well.

My set routine continued into the day of competition. It included arriving at a certain time before the event started and following the same warm-up procedure. The crucial part of my warm-up arrived when I put on my spikes or racing flats. Until this point I would enjoy the excitement of the event - jogging around with others and generally not trying to focus on what I was hoping to achieve.

About ten to fifteen minutes before the start, I would put on my spikes/racing flats to finish off my warm-up with some faster running. This point also served as the trigger for me to change to a different, more focused mental state. I would now reaffirm my goals and strategies, and begin to block out distractions that might interfere with my maintaining this race state of mind. I would now feel more detached from others and yet would seem fully alert to what was happening.

Perhaps my best athletic performance took place during a Master's Mile race in New York. Certainly it was the one that gave me the greatest thrill. I was so focused before the race that I couldn't find anything that was bothering me. No sore muscles or doubts about how well I might run - and yet I was running in Madisons Square Gardens before 18,000 people. It was a unique feeling. I finished second behind the Irish runner Eamon Coughlan who twice finished 4th in an Olympic final. My prize was a watch. After that I often would (and still do) wear the watch when I wanted to perform well. Putting on the watch brings back vivid memories of that night and I once again feel confident of what I can achieve.

3. MEANING

The third key of mental mastery is *meaning* - deciding what things *mean*.

I noted in an earlier chapter that you're *always* making decisions - each moment, you make decisions about what to focus your attention upon, and once you focus your attention, you then make a decision about what a particular thing or event *means* to you. For example, what does losing your keys; or someone smiling at you; or being cut off in traffic; or winning a match; or being late; or someone calling you a liar; or losing your job; mean?

For every event in your life, in order to understand and respond to it, you *have to give a meaning to it*. The important thing to realise is that these meanings are arbitrary - the meanings you give to events *become the meanings of these events for you*.

Meanings are choices : the meanings you give to events *become* the meanings of these events for you.

There is nothing that is inherently 'good' or 'bad' - it all depends on what you choose to make of it. A wonderful example of this was given by Denis Waitley in his *New Dynamics of Winning* audio tape, in which he tells the story of running late for an airline flight, and arriving just as they closed the flight. Despite his angry demands and pleas to the staff at the airport to hold the plane and let him on, they refuse. He decides to make a complaint to the management, and while he is waiting to do so, the news comes that the plane has crashed on take-off, killing everyone on board.

What was seen by him just a few moments ago as something to get angry and complain about, suddenly in an instant becomes something he is incredibly grateful for. I'm sure you can think of similar situations that have happened to you, in which something happened that you initially judged negatively, but which actually turned out to be to your benefit.

Every event that happens to you, you *have to* give a meaning to - good, bad, or indifferent. Because of this, the decisions you're making moment to moment about these meanings, determines whether you're an optimist or a pessimist. I covered this topic in detail in Chapter 6 of *Sportsmind*, and I'd like to add a few things to what I covered there.

SIX CHARACTERISTICS OF A POSITIVE ATTITUDE

Like every other behaviour, a positive mental attitude has a *specific structure* - there are specific things that people do, and a specific process they follow in their mind, in order to have a positive attitude.

The best such process description I've come across is that given by Steve Andreas and Charles Faulkner in *"NLP The New Technology of Achievement"*. They suggest that there are six vital characteristics that determine a positive mental attitude: Inner Motivation; High Standards; Self-to-Self Comparisons; Chunking Down Goals; Flexible Time Frames; and Personal Involvement.

There are six characteristics of a positive attitude.

As I go through each of these, you might reflect on how you rate in each category, recognising that no one characteristic is more important than another - and that a positive mental attitude is a result of the interaction of all of them.

Inner Motivation.
I've spoken about the difference between positive and negative motivation in the first chapter of *Sportsmind*: positive motivation being something that moves you *toward* what you want, while negative motivation moves you *away from* what you don't want. I also spoke of the importance, particularly for sportspeople, of encouraging more positive motivation in your life.

However, recent thinking suggests that maximum motivation is achieved by using *both* negative and positive forms of motivation.

Because many people are so used to motivating themselves negatively, in order to be most effective, first state what you *don't* want, and then state what you *do* want - in the same sentence.

Maximise motivation by using *both* forms: first state what you *don't* want, then state what you *do* want.

What is important is the sequence in which the negative and positive aspects of the directions are given. For instance, if I were giving instruction to a football or basketball team about improving on their defence, notice how *the order of what I say* influences your response. Which of these two statements is more appealing to you? :

"This time, let's start aggressively and maintain concentration throughout the entire match. No missed tackles, fumbles, or sloppy passing."

"This time, no missed tackles, fumbles, or sloppy passing. Let's start aggressively and maintain concentration throughout the entire match."

Most people find the *second statement* more useful, because you are made aware of what to avoid, and then given a positive direction or goal at the end - which is what remains most clearly in your mind. Of course, another alternative would be a pure positive motivation statement such as :

"This time, make every tackle, hold on to the ball, and pass accurately. Let's start aggressively and maintain concentration throughout the entire match."

CASE STUDY : Parenting

I've always thought I was as a very positively motivating person until I caught myself teaching my three year old son, Benjamin, to do certain things like clean his teeth after meals; put away his toys; etc. Rather than punishing him for not doing the 'right' thing, I'd been telling him *stories* about other little boys who *didn't* clean their teeth, or put their toys away - the stories usually ending in disaster for the boys displaying such 'bad' behaviours!

In other words, I was teaching him a classic negative motivation strategy! I realised this when he kept asking me to tell him stories of little boys who *didn't* do .... whatever!

Having a strong belief that encouraging people to develop a *wanting for the positive outcome* (positive motivation), rather than avoiding what they don't want (negative motivation), is a more useful motivation strategy, I changed my stories to be of the wonderful little boys who *did do* .... whatever, and of the positive consequences in their lives. It seems however, that even three year olds are fascinated by disaster - he still kept wanting to hear stories about the dreadful things that happened to the 'naughty' boys! So now I include a negative consequence, followed by a positive reward, in my stories!

In addition, what is equally important is that the motivation - either positive or negative - be fuelled by clearly defined, precise, and personal images of either the desired rewards or negative consequences. What this means is that, rather than having just a vague idea of what you want (positive motivation), or want to avoid (negative motivation), you identify *exactly* the negative consequences or the positive results of an action. Make the consequences and rewards more 'real' by using strong compelling submodalities in the way you picture and think about them.

High Standards and Self-to-Self Comparisons.
The next two characteristics of a positive mental attitude are a commitment to be your best - according to your own values, and compared only to your past self and future desired self, and not in relation to others.

Whenever you compare yourself with another athlete, student, salesperson, manager, parent, or whoever, you will find some that are 'better' and others that are 'worse' than you. Further, particularly in sports performance, if your self worth is based solely on comparison of yourself and your performances with others, then your confidence and self esteem will vary with your performance, and be unreliable.

If your self worth is based on comparing yourself to others, then your confidence will be unreliable.

On the other hand, if your self esteem is solidly based in your recognition of your ability to be better today than you were yesterday, and better tomorrow than you are today - then you can depend on yourself. You can trust in your confidence to be there when you need it, and know that you're worthy, regardless of whatever disasters, obstacles, challenges, problems, or setbacks that you face.

Certainly, look to other people's accomplishments and behaviours for inspiration; for specific ideas and techniques that work; and for the thinking and feeling strategies of successful people that you can model - but look only to yourself for measurements of progress and worth. Do this by regularly asking: "In what areas have I improved, and by how much, compared to who I was yesterday, or last year, or ten years ago?"

Chunking Down Goals and Flexible Time Frames.
The next two characteristics of a positive mental attitude are firstly the ability to break down big goals into achievable steps and action plans; and having the ability to change your perception of time. I discussed goals and goal achieving in great detail in Chapter 3, and I will be looking in greater detail at your perception and mastery of time, and time frames, when I discuss the fourth and final key of mental mastery.

Suffice it to say that, as with the perceptual shifts of first, second, and third position which I discussed earlier in this chapter, there are *time perceptions* which champions use, and vary, according to need - and which assist in the achievement of their goals.

> **Champions have the ability to vary their perception of time according to need, to accomplish their goals.**

Personal Involvement.
The final characteristic which Andreas and Faulkner identify is that of your ability to take *personal responsibility* for your own performances - to be an active player in designing your own future. Individuals with a positive mental attitude are not passive, or overly aggressive, but show a determined involvement and care about, whatever they choose to do - be it a sporting activity, a career, or being a parent.

Recognise that you are not a victim of circumstances - there is no 'luck' except that won through personal effort and commitment.

> **Champions know that the harder you train, the 'luckier' you become!**

LANGUAGE

One final element of the structure of a positive mental attitude is the *language* you use in ascribing meanings to events in your life. For example if you call an event a *disaster*, (eg. losing your job, your partner leaving you, or a stock market crash), the word itself brings with it a particular *intensity* of response. The result of using that specific language, is that you won't feel very empowered to deal with the situation.

However, if you label that same event as a minor setback, a correction, a slight 'glitch', or some such language, then those words generate an entirely different response. You feel more able to handle the challenge, and weather it successfully.

The specific language labels you use for events, affects how you respond to those events.

If your partner leaves you, or if you lose a job, or lose an important match, then you have a choice about how you describe and label those events - and these labels provide the meaning of the events to you. If you say, "They left me because I'm not attractive", or "I lost my job because I'm not good enough", then you're probably not going to handle the setback very well. Yet if you said "Now I have an opportunity to find someone who's really right for me", or "Now I have more time for my family and to find a job in that career I've been wanting to move into", then you'll feel empowered to take positive action.

Negative attitudes and labels make you see doom and gloom and feel disempowered to act, while a positive attitude and labels generate pictures of possibility and solutions, and empowers you.

4. TIMING

The final key to mental mastery is learning how to master time, and timing. There are three issues that I want to discuss here: Time Management; Perceptual Time Shifts; and Timing.

Time Management.
Time management relates to how effective you are in the day-to-day managing of your time: how you plan and organise your activities, and how efficient you are in your use of time.

Your most valuable commodity is time.

It's been said that the most valuable commodity we have is *time*. You can always earn more money, or get a new job, or a new partner, or replace a smashed car, or a lost wallet - but you can never get one more second of time. Yet many people act as if they were immortal, frittering away time on inane activities and 'pastimes', (what a *dreadful* word that is!), apparently unaware that at any moment Death may reach out and take them.

One of the most empowering ideas I've ever come across, (borrowed from the books of Carlos Castaneda), is to continually hold an awareness of your impending death, as a mechanism for bringing power and focus into what you do in your life. Nothing motivates you, I believe, more than the recognition of your own mortality, and the uncertainty of when Death will take you!

Unfortunately, in our society death is something that is rarely seen; there is little opportunity to establish an understanding of and a 'relationship' with the idea of your own death. Such a relationship lends you and your actions a sense of immediacy, clarity, and power than cannot be attained in any other way.

Someone acting in their life with a full awareness of their imminent demise can act without fear or favour - for what do they have to lose? Far from being morbid, as some people have suggested, I find this practice enlightening and empowering, and provides a means for cutting through all the unimportant 'dross' of merely existing, to design a life of worth.

If you find yourself hesitating, or feeling stuck or bored, then think for a moment of your death.

So if you find yourself hesitating, or doubting yourself, or feeling stuck or bored : take a moment to stop, glance over your left shoulder, and catch a fleeting glimpse of the dark shadow that will one day claim you. Use this glimpse to empower you and spur you to live and do what is in your heart to accomplish here.

As I explained in the earlier section on *Inner Motivation*, it's important to make this concept of your own death 'real' in your mind, rather than just some vague notion. Certainly, put it a long way into the future, but do recognise that one day, you *will* cease to exist - at least in the form you currently inhabit!

This concept also reinforces the importance of having a life purpose, or mission for your life, as discussed in Chapter 2. Regardless of what your beliefs may be about any supposed 'after-life', having such a life mission provides an immediate and verifiable sense of purpose, as opposed to that of merely blind 'faith' in a 'heaven' or 'hell'.

You can also fully participate in life, and provide something of worth to your community *in the here and now*, rather than just 'preparing to live' in some hoped for, and uncertain, 'after-life'.

ORGANISING YOURSELF

Time management also means organising yourself, so you have not only the passion and desire to succeed, but also the wherewithal. What this means in practice is simply two things: condensing your life to three or four key areas; and the ability to keep your 'attention' clear.

Condense your life to three or four key areas.

Many people fail to succeed simply because they attempt too many things. If you want to succeed at a high level in anything, it requires a significant commitment of time and effort - but if you're spread too thin, you'll be unable to achieve this. So I suggest that you 'condense' your life to three or four key areas, and let the rest go. For example, my key areas are my family; my *Sportsmind* Vision; my sport of Aikido; and my small acreage of permaculture. I would dearly love to take up volleyball and golf again, and maybe complete a doctorate, but I know that if I did, I'd just end up taking time from one of those other areas - which is something I'm not willing to do.

So what are the key areas in your life? Take ten minutes now to identify these, and condense your life to those most important.

Keeping your attention clear means simply *doing the jobs* - not leaving 'unfinished business' around. It could be said that you have only a given number of 'units of attention' before you get overwhelmed. Every bit of unfinished business takes up your attention and mental energy, and prevents you from doing something else. In order to fully focus you energies, it's important to have all your circuits clear.

This is vital, particularly to elite sportspeople. I heard Tom Lehman interviewed about his preparation for a golf tournament, and his need to have everything organised to allow him to feel prepared. Likewise, I've found the same need with a lot of the elite athletes I've worked with - once you're organised, you can relax and focus on the task of putting in your best performance.

Once you're organised, you can relax and focus on the task of putting in your best performance.

A good example of what can happen if you don't get organised was given by a small bore rifle shooter, who told me the story of being in the middle of a competition when she suddenly wondered, "Did I leave the iron on?" Needles to say, her concentration was completely 'shot' from then on! (Excuse pun)

The unfinished business I'm speaking of here is not just unanswered correspondence or outstanding work you've been putting off, but can take many forms. For example, it can be something broken that you've been 'meaning to get fixed'; old clothes or junk in the garage you've yet to throw away; a book or something else borrowed from a friend you've failed to return; or even an agreement with someone to do something that you haven't yet lived up to.

An excellent way to clear your attention so that you can fully focus on what's really important, is to have a thorough cleanup, at home and at your work. Think of it this way: if you have a glass, and it's currently full of water, you can't put any new water in - until you tip out the old water. While your attention is 'full' of unfinished business, you won't be able to 'fill up' with any more success, until you resolve the unfinished business.

THE IMPORTANCE OF RELEASE

In order to become more successful, in any area, requires some kind of behavioural change. *If you keep doing what you've always done, you'll continue to get what you've always got.* So understanding how to change behaviours is a vital key to being successful. The single most important, and often unrecognised, key to change is simply *release*.

Before any change can occur, a release is needed.

Recognise that your *physical* environment is a reflection of what's going on *inside* you - so cleaning up on the outside will help to focus and clarify your thoughts and goals. When you release and let go of old possessions and behaviours, you empty your cup and open yourself to receive what is right for you *now*. The following exercise can be used to clear some space in yourself, and in your life, and is a precursor to the next chapter on changing beliefs.

EXERCISE : A Personal Clean-up

1. Set aside some time over the next two weeks to have a big physical clean-up. Go through your house, garage, office, desk, filing cabinet, etc. and throw away what is no longer of use or importance to you. Tidy what is important and organise it so you know where to find it.
2. When completed, take 15 minutes to consider your current behaviours, attitudes, and beliefs. Which of these are no longer serving you? Write them down on a piece of paper, and underneath each one write: "I now release this behaviour/attitude/belief about ....", and then throw the piece of paper away with all the other rubbish from your clean-up.

Perceptual Time Shifts.

Perceptual time shifts relate to your ability to change from a past, to a present, or to a future perspective in relation to time. Elite performers in every field have the ability to be fully present in the moment *when they're actually performing*; to review a past performance or collection of performances in order to identify areas of improvement; and to also clearly see and associate to future plans and desired goals to achieve them.

Champions can focus on the present, past and future.

Shifting your time perception is similar to shifting within first, second, and third positions which I discussed earlier. The easiest way to learn to make such time shifts is to utilise the concept of *timelines*, (see *Sportsmind*). Recognise also that there is a relationship between your ability to shift to third position, for instance, and your ability to take a past or future perspective - so if you haven't successfully completed the exercise from page 164, I encourage you to do so, before doing the following exercise.

EXERCISE : Present, Past and Future Perspectives
1. Using the strategy outlined in *Sportsmind*, elicit your past and future timeline, and picture it in some concrete way. Eg. you might imagine it as a road, or a stream, or a thread, etc.
2. Beginning with a sense of being fully associated and present in the moment, imagine lifting up out of your body to third position, still in the present - looking down on yourself, and also seeing your past and future timeline.
3. Explore your timeline: go back into the past, floating above your timeline, then forward into the future, before returning to your body in the present. Reflect on your experience.

The above exercise is particularly helpful in identifying and releasing negative 'frog soup' patterns in your life. From third position, above your past timeline, you can look back and see what patterns of behaviours and beliefs that you've maintained - and the desirable or undesirable consequences of these beliefs and behaviours on your life, and performance. You can also look through the present to the future to recognise that if you don't *change now*, then a negative pattern will continue to repeat itself.

Timing.

The best way to speak of timing is to use an example from Aikido. When someone attacks you, there is a moment in which they gather their energy prior to expending it in the form of an attack. So there is a very small window of opportunity prior to an attack, in which you can take control of the situation. This is identified *physically* in the person attacking by their taking an 'in-breath'. Before we can expend energy, we have to first gather energy in. Try it yourself - draw back your fist and arm as if you were going to punch someone, and notice how as you do, it's natural to take a breath in. Then you expel it as you punch.

However, this concept doesn't just apply to combat - in order to achieve anything, to do anything, there is a period of gathering of energy first - then the expenditure of energy. For example, think of a tennis forehand or a golf swing - you first take back the club or racquet in order to develop the power to hit the ball. Also in Nature, and even in business, there are periods of withdrawal prior to bursts of growth or activity - eg. Winter, then Spring.

The idea for the Aikido exponent is to be aware of the movement of 'energy' in your partner, (through attention to their breathing and other non-verbal signals), and to blend with their attack at the point *just prior to it happening*, so as to re-direct their movement and energy to your purpose.

However it's not just the physical action that happens in someone attacking - a worthy opponent will also attack with their *mind*. So timing certainly means taking action to 'catch' my opponent's arm or wrist in that window of opportunity before the completion of their in-breath and their attack, but it also means 'capturing' their mind; to blend with their attack at the point of *intention*.

You recall I spoke in an earlier chapter about the 'choice point of thought' within us? What I do when I 'capture my opponent's mind' is to enter into their thought space and take control of that choice point of thought - in them. So that just as they intend an action, I've already blended with that intention and turned it in another direction. While this may sound esoteric, I'm sure you've already experienced it, many times. Every time you've competed or interacted with someone and been able to somehow *know* - beyond logic - what they were going to do, is an example of this.

To some the concept of 'capturing your opponents mind' may seem dishonourable, or even 'evil'. If this is the case, let me ask you two questions: Firstly, if it's OK to compete and struggle against someone *physically* during the game, why is it different to apply such mental pressure? Why is it OK to compete physically, but not mentally? Secondly, when does the actual competition begin? Does it begin when the officials blow the whistle to begin, or while you're warming up, or when you first step onto the playing field? Many people think of a competition starting at the 'official' starting time of the first serve, or play, or whatever - but I would argue that it begins days, or even weeks before.

Also you may have been on the receiving end of the process! If you've ever felt totally controlled by someone else, or totally unconfident around them to the point where you're not acting or performing in your normal manner - they've captured your mind; or rather, you've *allowed* them to capture your intention point.

EXERCISE : Capturing Your Opponent's Mind

1. Using the format I outlined in the *Sportsmind* audio tapes, do a relaxation and build a 'positive bubble' for yourself.

2. In a similar way to how you modelled the behaviour of someone you admire, this time picture your opponent, go to second position and associate into them: get a feel for how they move, what they see, and what they hear or say to themselves when they're playing / performing.

3. Now simply intend to capture their intention - to know their plans, strategies and intentions.

4. Return to yourself and reflect on the exercise.

CASE STUDY : Cyclist

The above exercise is excellent for taking charge in a competitive interaction - *and you will also want to know how to shield yourself against it, if someone applies it to you*! A professional female cyclist asked me for some help in dealing with a situation in which her opponent was staring her down just prior to the start of a race - and this was putting her off.

Through using the 'positive bubble' process (outlined in detail in the *Sportsmind* audio tapes) she was able to block her opponent's attempts to psych her out, and shield herself from her influence.

The final aspect of timing that's important, particularly to athletes, is the ability to 'stop' or 'stretch' time - similar to what happens when you experience a life threatening incident and everything, apparently, slows down. I'm sure you've recognised the ability of elite sportspeople to apparently have so much time to get into position and play their shots. Essentially what they're doing is stopping time. This is a fascinating topic, but it relates very much to some ideas I'm going to present in my next book on *Sports Hypnosis* so I'll discuss it in further detail there.

"You are a champion because you like yourself — knowing that it's not what other people say that matters, it's what you say to yourself."

CHAPTER 7 :

NO
LIMITS

INTERNAL INGREDIENTS OF SUCCESS

Learning to change your *behaviour* is a key ingredient in success. Any behavioural change - whether it be an athlete aiming to perform at a higher level, or an individual's decision to give up smoking - first happens in the *minds* of those involved.

Often, the emphasis in our striving for improvement is placed on the *external* ingredients - the new procedures or techniques to be learned, the different communication practices, or the altered diet or lifestyle. Yet to be effective, change wants to first be directed to the *mindset* of the individual, team or organisation involved - to change the limiting *beliefs* that support the existing behaviours.

Champions understand the importance of beliefs, and consistently nurture positive, peak performance beliefs in themselves and those around them.

BELIEFS : BORDER GUARDS OF THE PERSONALITY

Our beliefs *define and constrain who we are*. I call beliefs the *border guards of the personality*, because they both limit and empower us by defining the boundaries of who we are and how we behave. Your beliefs establish the edges of 'you' and 'not-you'.

And of course we're all continually reinforcing those boundaries with our thinking, and our responses to events and circumstances throughout the day: "I couldn't do *that*"; "It's not *right* to allow people to ... whatever"; "I love doing this"; "That's a great idea"; "This is too hard"; "She's just like me"; "That's stupid"; "I'm not very good at ... whatever"; "I agree with you";   and so on.

Your beliefs define the edges of your personality.

However, our beliefs are not just harmless ideas or emotions - they are so powerful that they can even affect us *physically*. One of the most astounding studies I ever heard about, which demonstrates this power of beliefs, was done by Professor Bernie Siegel from Yale university. He has worked extensively with people who have multiple personality disorders - ie. they believe they are many different people, and these different people have discrete and very different personalities. Professor Siegel found that these peoples' beliefs that they had become a totally different person was so powerful it resulted in *measurable physiological changes in their bodies*, as well as psychological changes.

Patients' *eye colour* actually changed as their personality changed; chronic illnesses like hypertension and diabetes came and went; and physical markings on their bodies appeared and disappeared *depending on the person's belief about 'who' they were!*

BELIEFS AND HEALING

Beliefs can also affect your ability to get well when you're sick. Have you ever heard of the term 'placebo'? A placebo is usually a simple sugar pill with no active ingredients which is used as a control in scientific studies on the effectiveness of pharmaceutical drugs. So in an experiment with 1000 people, 500 people might be given the drug and the other 500 given a placebo.

Because most drugs are tested against placebos in this way, there's a lot of scientific literature about their effects. The interesting thing is that sometimes the people taking the placebo show more positive effects than the people given the drugs!

Placebos can have more impact than the drugs!

How can this be? Simply through the process of the patients believing the 'medicine' they are being given will work.

Similarly, Dr. Carl Simonton and others such as Ian Gawler have used the power of their patients' beliefs, (through the use of relaxation and visualisation techniques), to cure diseases such as hypertension and cancer. Dr. Gerald Jampolsky has likewise used a belief change process, (again with the use of visualisation techniques), in work with remedial reading students to increase their progress by two-and-a-half times in a little over two months!

Such visualisation processes, (which rely on belief to work), have also been used to reduce the healing time of sports injuries and to maintain form - a golfer I know who broke her hand visualised playing while she had it in plaster for six weeks, then on her first match back, hit a course record and won a big tournament!

WHAT IS A BELIEF?

I've been looking at and talking about beliefs, but what exactly are these things we call beliefs, that can be so powerful in our lives?

Basically, a belief is simply *a decision about what something means*, and it's supported by what are known as internal or external *references*: by internal mental constructs, or by external life experiences which support that belief.

A belief is *a decision about what something means*, and are built from internal or external references.

For instance, Anthony Robbins suggests we think of an idea as a table top without legs - there's nothing to support that idea; nothing to hold it up. However, that idea becomes a *belief* when you start to put legs under the table top to support it. The more 'legs' you put under the table, the more 'solid' it is, and the more *certain* you are about that belief being 'true'.

These 'legs' of a belief are known as *references* - and they may be either internal thoughts, or external life experiences that support that belief. An example of *external* references are things like life experiences - something outside of you that supports a particular belief.

For example, you might go out to play your very first game of golf, and when you first go to drive the ball off the tee, you slice it so it veers way off to the right into the trees. And the same happens on every drive you do. Pretty soon you can start to build up a belief which says "I always slice", and its a strong belief because it's supported by external experiences of doing so.

However, the legs of your table of belief can also be *internal* references - mental constructs of your own that aren't necessarily supported by external experiences. For instance, have you ever known someone who honestly believed they were good at something, even though the external feedback didn't support that belief? That's called 'being a legend in your own mind'!

Now while that might be amusing, its important to understand that *strong internal references, that are not necessarily supported by external life experiences are very important to succeed when engaging in a new activity of some kind.*

Strong *internal* references are necessary to succeed.

For example, learning a musical instrument or a foreign language, or a new computer program; competing at a higher grade or level than previously (eg Olympics); starting a business for the first time; having a baby for the first time; changing your career or job to something you've never done before; your first day at university; your first sexual relationship; and so on.

Once you've done it once or twice, most people generally feel relatively confident about doing something again, and it's relatively easy compared to the first time isn't it? (Although, there *are* people who actually have *negative* internal references even though they have received positive external success and support. That's called lacking confidence *in* yourself - ie. an *internal* reference of confidence)

To succeed at something you've never done before, you first want to build strong *internal* reference of success - because you don't have any previous *external* ones, do you?

Isn't this what we do with our kids when we first send them to school? We tell them what a great time they're going to have, and how they're going to make lots of friends, and do heaps of interesting things - so they build up a sense of *internal confidence* about doing well at school. Yet do we do that with ourselves?

For your to act with confidence and competence in any activity, you will want to have lots of 'legs' under your table top of belief - because *the body cannot do what the mind won't believe.*

The body cannot do what the mind won't believe.

A wonderful example of this was the eventual breaking of the four-minute mile 'barrier'. Prior to 1954, it was considered 'impossible' for a human to run the mile in under four minutes - no one had been able to do it, and physiologists suggested that the body would overheat; that it was physiologically impossible. However in 1954 a man by the name of Roger Bannister did the 'impossible' - he ran the mile in a time of 3.59.4. Later that same year, John Landy broke it twice, and Bannister also did it again. In the next three years, the four minute 'barrier' was broken no less than 25 times by 15 different runners - and of course many more times since then.

The difference between someone who uses this process intelligently and the deluded person who is a 'legend in their own mind', is that they build strong internal references (I can do this), and they clearly and strongly visualise themselves succeeding - then they go out and try it. However they also have an *external check* to analyse their performance and change their approach *until* they achieve the success they want - *and without losing that strong internal reference of success.*

SELECTIVE PERCEPTION

You can develop a belief about *anything* provided you can build enough legs, ie. internal and /or external references, to support it! I'm sure you've heard the statement that most of your adult beliefs and attitudes were programmed into you by the time you were just seven or eight years old - before you even developed enough experience and knowledge to question or challenge them! This means that most people are simply reacting to the world based on beliefs that they've just accepted as true, and never really tested.

Most of our adult beliefs / attitudes were programmed into us by the time we were seven or eight years old.

I wonder what beliefs you're currently holding that were programmed in while you were too young to question them? Do you have any negative or limiting beliefs that are preventing you from reaching your full potential? What areas of your life are currently not working for you? Could your beliefs in this area be causing the problems?

It's important to recognise that once you accept a belief as 'true', then you automatically and unconsciously act to make it true, and will *selectively block out information to the contrary.* For instance, read the following sentence, and count how many letter f's there are. Do this now before reading further.

EXERCISE : Count the F's

Scientific findings are the result of the collaboration of numerous researchers from different countries and institutions, and the experience of many years.

How many f's did you find? And how much would you be willing to bet that you're correct? Quickly read it again and make sure, before reading on.

If you're like the majority of people you would have found five, or perhaps six, f's in that sentence. Now go back and read it again, and this time include the f's in the word 'of' as well. In reality there are actually eight 'f's' in that sentence, aren't there! This is not a particularly difficult task, yet it's surprising how many people miss the f's in the 'of's'. How does this happen?

The reason is that when you read, the word 'of' is pronounced as 'ov', and you literally don't see it because you've decided based on your subvocalisation that there is no 'f' there! Of course if you read the sentence backwards, or went through a letter at a time you would have obtained the correct answer. If you did this, try it on some other people, and be surprised at how they miss some!

Despite the reality that was right before your eyes, you unconsciously misperceived something different!

In other words, your *belief* about the sound of the 'of' as being 'ov', was so strong, you literally couldn't see the f's that were right in front of your eyes! I've done this exercise with hundreds of people, and before telling them the answer, I've asked them to re-read the sentence five or six times; I've even had other people beside them get different answers - and still they persist in their belief that they have the correct number, until I show them! In fact, I play a little game of 'how much would you bet that you're correct?' If I was an unscrupulous person, I'd be very wealthy now, since most people have bet at least $1,000.00 that their answers were correct!

THE SELF IMAGE AND BELIEFS

So do recognise that your beliefs are not necessarily based on logic, common sense, or even on 'truth' or 'reality'! Too often our beliefs are a result of powerful emotional experiences that we had as a child - and you may well be basing decisions and actions in your life on *misinformation*, on beliefs that are no longer useful for you, because you've missed a few f's along the way!

I introduced a simple behavioural model in the *Sportsmind* book, in which I showed how your behaviours and performances are influenced by your self image - how we must act like the person we *imagine* ourselves to be. You literally cannot act otherwise; you must act out your self image of yourself. Someone who sees themselves as a slow starter will be a slow starter, someone who sees themselves as honest would find it difficult to lie, and so on.

> **You must act like the person you imagine yourself to be - you must be true to your self image.**

This process of acting out your self image happens totally unconsciously - you don't have to remember to be you do you? You don't wake up in the morning and say to yourself, "I have to remember to be myself today"! It just happens automatically - you're just you. You know how you respond to certain people and events in your life; you know what kinds of food you eat, the kind of work you do, and the leisure activities you engage in.

Beliefs work in the same way. In fact, your self image is simply a collection of beliefs about yourself - beliefs you've collected over the years, taking on the comments of your parents, teachers, coaches, friends, and peers to build an identity of 'who' you are.

So it doesn't matter whether a belief is 'true' or not, or even whether it's beneficial or detrimental to you - you will still act *as if* it was true! In just the same way that you were willing to bet money on your 'knowing' you had the correct number of f's!

If you believe that you're not as good as someone else; that you don't have the talent or the connections to succeed - then you won't. If you believe that learning is difficult; or that you never play bunkers well; or that you've got a weak backhand ..... then that's precisely what you'll manifest, and you will block out anything that is counter to your beliefs, even if it's 'true'. Just like you blocked out seeing all the f's - even though they were there.

You can re-decide about a belief, any time you want.

Because you automatically and unconsciously act out your beliefs, it's important to recognise and understand two things. Firstly, because beliefs are choices - simple decisions that you've made about something - *you can re-decide about any belief, any time you want to*. Most people don't recognise this, and act as if their beliefs were objectively 'true', rather than just choices they made. As a consequence, they are operating totally unconsciously from their beliefs, and which are rarely questioned.

Secondly, make sure the beliefs that you do choose for yourself are positive and empowering beliefs that accurately reflect your full potential in your work, sport and personal life. Think for a few moments: what would you *like* to believe about yourself? What would you *rather believe* than some of the limiting and negative beliefs you currently hold? What *could* you believe that would be more useful and empowering - particularly in those challenging situations?

TRUE LIES

There is a wonderful story, attributed to Abraham Maslow, which illustrates how we like to hold on to our beliefs. The story is about a psychiatrist who was treating a patient who believed he was a corpse, and despite numerous therapy sessions and all the logical arguments of the psychiatrist, the man continued to claim he was dead. Then in a flash of inspiration the psychiatrist asked him, "Do corpses bleed?", to which his patient responded, "Of course not!" So the psychiatrist pulls out a pin and pricks the man's thumb with it, which of course started to bleed. Looking on expectantly, the psychiatrist waits for the patient's response. The patient looks down at his bleeding thumb, and says "Well, what do you know. Corpses do bleed!"

Which just goes to show that people like to hold on to their beliefs - even in the face of counter evidence!

Ask yourself : is this belief *useful* in my life?

The way I like to think about beliefs now is not in terms of whether a particular belief is 'true' or 'right', but rather, is it *useful* for me in my life? If I believe this particular belief, and I act on it, what effects does it have on me, and on my performance?

No belief is inherently 'true' or 'right' - you can only honestly evaluate a belief in terms of its *outcomes* in your life. Rather than seeking beliefs that are 'true', I now evaluate a belief on its effects - on its outcome in my life, and whether I'm comfortable with that or not. Ask, what does this belief do for me? Does it empower me, or limit me? Does it add something of value to me and the people important to me, or does it cause problems?

The trouble with seeking true/false beliefs is that we're learning so much so rapidly now that virtually everything you and I were taught in school is now outdated and 'wrong'.

A wonderful example of this is given by recent findings in physics, which have shown that the model of the atom which I learned in school - of a central nucleus with electrons whirling around it - is no longer an accurate representation of 'reality'. The 'reality' is more like a 'hologram', apparently - but that didn't stop them from splitting the atom! Another example is that given by light - which acts like either a particle, or a wave - *depending on the observer!*

Aren't there beliefs that you used to hold and defend passionately, that you now no longer believe?

It's the same with personal beliefs about ourselves. Aren't there beliefs that you used to hold and passionately defend at one time, that you now no longer believe - and you might even be embarrassed to admit that you thought that way? For example, what about Santa and the Easter Bunny? I remember I used to believe so strongly in the Easter Bunny that one day, (as a three year old!), I actually saw it! Now that's a powerful belief!

Aren't there ways of training, or dietary patterns that you used to believe were beneficial, that you now know are not so good? What about relationships - how our beliefs about what is a 'family' have changed over the past twenty years! What about beliefs about what's possible? Who, ten years ago, would have thought that a 36 year old man would be the world champion in the 100 meter dash? Lindford Christie certainly did when he took the crown in 1996!

It can be very self empowering, and perhaps a little scary for some people, to get to the point where you recognise and accept that *all* your beliefs are just that - beliefs. Simply decisions that you've made, and that *none of them are inherently true!*

It's empowering because once you accept the fact that all your beliefs are choices - you can go through them, and using the belief change processes I will show you, change the ones you don't like and replace them with more useful, powerful beliefs!

The first step in this process is to develop an awareness of your current beliefs - both positive and negative beliefs. Use the following exercise to develop an awareness of your current beliefs, and learn how to change the limiting ones.

EXERCISE : Limiting and Empowering Beliefs

1. Identify Your Current Negative and Positive Beliefs.
Write down on a sheet of paper a list of your current beliefs: note all those that disempower and limit you on one side of the paper, and on the other side write down all those that strengthen and empower you.

For example, some negative beliefs might include things like : I'm not a morning person; Learning is difficult; I'm not smart enough; I'm a slow starter; Failure is bad; It takes a long time to reach the top; Only a few people can succeed; People don't like me; etc. Positive beliefs might include things like : I always play well under pressure; I'm a happy person, I never let things get me down; I eat healthy food and look after my body; I never give up, I'm a fighter; I'm always improving and learning from others; Failure is feedback; Learning is easy and fun; I've got time; etc.

2. Note Your Most Empowering Beliefs.

Take a few minutes to review your positive beliefs, and then circle the ones that are *the most empowering* to you. Think about how these beliefs strengthen and help you. Identify *times and places in your future* where you want to have a very strong awareness of these positive empowering beliefs, and note them down.

3. Challenge the Limiting Beliefs.

Now circle the most limiting beliefs - the ones that hold you back the most - and consider the consequences of them in your life. Feel the pain they're causing you. Imagine how good it would be if you didn't have those beliefs. Think of the positive consequences to your life of letting them go now.

Challenge them by asking yourself the following questions about these disempowering beliefs:
Who did I learn it from? Were they succeeding in their life in a way I want to emulate? Do I want to be like that?
What will it cost me if I don't change this belief soon?
How is this belief wrong? Look for logical flaws in the belief, and times it <u>wasn't</u> true. Think of examples of people who believe the exact opposite. What references do they use?

4. Design New Beliefs.

What would you <u>rather</u> believe? What are you going to replace those limiting beliefs with? If you have trouble with this, think "What would I have to believe in this situation in order to get what I want?" Or you may want to model someone who is already successful in this area and think about what they believe that helps them to succeed. If you don't know, ask yourself, "If I did know, what would it be?" Ensure you have a replacement for every limiting belief listed.

208

CASE STUDY : Female Rower

I was speaking to a rowing coach who told me of an exceptionally talented young female rower of his who had everything going for her - yet she kept under-achieving. He finally discovered that deep down this girl had a belief, (instilled by her mother at an early age), that "girls should never do anything to get themselves sweaty"! Of course, this belief caused a great conflict within her, and prevented her from really putting in a full 100% effort - because she felt she was being 'bad' getting so sweaty!

Of course, the next question people ask is : "How can just changing your belief about something change your ability and performance? If you've always sliced, and you now change your belief to that you hit straight down the fairway, will you change?" The answer is yes, and let me explain it in this way. Let's use "I always slice" as an example. Of course simply changing an internal reference of a belief as we have done, (from "I always slice" to something like "I hit the fairway nine out of ten times"), still leaves the external reality to be dealt with. So you will still want to put in effort to practice and improve your golf swing, or whatever - but consider the alternative.

If you keep your internal negative belief the same, ("I always slice"), then you'll *never* get better, because you'll unconsciously open the club face on impact to maintain your 'self image' of being a slicer. The same process works, but in reverse, for someone with a positive belief - the belief will provide the impetus to make their behaviour match up with their self image. Recognise that the self image dictates behaviour and performance - change your self image and you change your performance. The process of changing your belief will not only give you a more positive self image, but will also provide the motivation to change. You will *want to* practice and improve to maintain your new belief, and you will do this unconsciously and naturally.

THE STRUCTURE OF BELIEF

I've mentioned many times already in this book that all behaviours have a *structure*, or a mental program which enables us to 'operate' that behaviour. (If there is one thing I want you to remember and take from this book, it is this principle!) Likewise, all beliefs have a structure; all decisions have a structure.

You will also recall, from Chapter Five, that I identified three 'building blocks' of emotional states: physiology, ideology and environment. The 'building blocks' of belief are similar to those I described for ideology - ie. the particular visual, auditory, and kinaesthetic 'thoughts' you have, and the specific submodality distinctions you make in these thoughts.

> **Beliefs have a structure : your visual, auditory, and kinaesthetic 'thoughts' and their submodalities.**

In other words, to create a belief about something you need to picture something (with specific submodalities); hear or say something to yourself (with specific submodalities); and feel something (with specific submodalities).

A belief *is* simply a collection of images, thoughts, and feelings that we experience, and which we attach to a particular behaviour called 'believing'. Of course, this is a pretty important behaviour, because *all of your day to day decisions* are based on first referring to particular beliefs about the world, or yourself, before any action is taken.

For example, to create a belief that you were unattractive to the opposite sex, what might you imagine, say, and feel?

Of course, if you pictured asking someone out and you imagined them laughing at you, and rejecting you - and you saw this picture big, bright, colourful and up close; and you said to yourself in a despondent low tone of voice close to your right ear, "No one likes me, I'm not very attractive"; and you felt a sinking, nauseous feeling in your stomach, and a flushing in your face every time you went to talk to someone .... then this could very well create a belief of unattractiveness to the opposite sex!

Now as with all internal processes, it's not just the *content* of your thoughts that is important, but the specific submodalities you use in your thinking. The content is of course important to some degree, but *how* you think about an issue is even more significant in it's influence upon your feelings and your behaviour.

The content of your thoughts is not as important as *how* you think - the specific submodalities you use.

You will recall from Chapter 4 when I spoke on goal setting, I stressed the importance of using powerful submodalities to make them compelling - picturing your goals big, bright, close, colourful, 3-D movies for maximum effect. The submodalities you use in your thinking are very significant. For example, do you have an internal critical voice? Remember a time you criticised yourself. Criticise yourself now for something, and listen to the specific auditory submodalities you use. Which direction does your voice originate from? How loud is it? What is its tone and tempo like? Now keep the content the same, but change the tone of your critical voice to be like Demi Moore's voice, and make it softer, and slower. Now make it sound like Donald Duck, increase the tempo, and have it come from a different place. Notice how these changes change your response!

SUBMODALITY FAMILIARISATION

Having the ability to identify the specific *submodality structure* of someone's thinking, is an incredibly valuable tool for understanding how they do what they do - both in working out how they might be creating a problem for themselves, and also in appreciating how they achieve excellence in a particular task. If you want to be able to do what someone else can do, the first step is to model the structure of their thinking processes.

Of course, you also want to be able to understand and specify the structure of *your own thinking* - both to work out how to change negative limiting beliefs or behaviours, and to reinforce your positive, empowering beliefs and behaviours.

> **If you want to be able to do what a champion can do, model the structure of their thinking processes.**

I spoke very briefly about submodalities in the *Sportsmind* book, and provided a list of some common visual, auditory, and kinaesthetic submodalities to be aware of. However, this is such an important area of peak performance psychology that it's vital to familiarise yourself more fully with it - particularly before I talk about how to change, or create, beliefs.

The easiest way to identify submodality details in your own thinking is to compare and contrast two experiences or memories. Use the following exercise to compare and contrast the submodality differences between a time you performed 'averagely' and a time you performed 'very well' in a particular task or activity. This will enable you to familiarise yourself with the submodalities you use in your thinking.

EXERCISE : Contrasting Submodalities

Identify an activity that you sometimes perform averagely, and sometimes do very well. Contrast submodalities of each.

	Average	Well
Visual		
Location / Distance		
Number of Images		
Size and Shape		
Moving / Still		
Colour / B&W		
Brightness		
Associated / Dissociated		
3D / Flat		
Bordered / Panoramic		
Auditory		
Location / Distance		
Words / Noise / Music		
Content [Describe]		
Loudness and Clarity		
Tone / Pitch		
Speed and Rhythm		
Kinaesthetic		
Location / Extent		
Pressure and Texture		
Temperature		
Moisture		
Moving / Still		
Rhythm		
Intensity and Duration		
Smells or Tastes		

CHANGING BELIEFS

To change a negative or limiting belief, the task is to simply *change some part of its structure, and the whole belief changes!* Change the submodalities in some way, and you change the belief. So the first step is to identify the submodality structure of a belief. For example, let's consider our golfer with the "I always slice" belief. This belief may have the following structure:

Visual = half a dozen images of my golf ball slicing off to the right; the images are big and close; it's a movie, in colour; normal daytime brightness; I am associated in the image; it's 3-D and panoramic (no border).
Auditory = No external sounds, but I'm saying to myself, "Damn, there I go again". This comes from just behind my right ear, in a clear, loud voice and an angry, frustrated tone. Normal talking speed, no special rhythm.
Kinaesthetic = A feeling of tightness in my shoulders, and a frown on my face, and tension around my forehead. Breathing is faster, and there is also a sinking feeling experienced in my stomach. This feeling is intense at first, and then diminishes slowly. No moisture, texture, or temperature differences.

To change a negative or limiting belief, simply change some part of its structure - ie. the submodalities used.

Do recognise that the belief is *precisely this process the person uses*. Every time he thinks about his ability as a golfer, the above 'program' operates, he identifies with it, and so 'believes' it. This identification with a particular belief, or behaviour, is the key. Once you say to yourself, "That's like me", or "That's not like me", this either locks the belief in place, or begins to weaken it.

Understanding this process of identifying or dis-identifying with a particular belief, can help you to both change those beliefs that are not serving you well, and to reinforce the positive and useful beliefs you hold.

Use the following exercise to change a negative, limiting belief. What belief would you like to change? Go back to the *Limiting and Empowering Beliefs* exercise you did earlier in this chapter - what beliefs do you need to let go of? Choose one of these to work with in the following exercise.

<u>EXERCISE : Changing a Negative Belief</u>

1. Identify *Strong* and *Weak* Beliefs
Using the *submodalities* list, compare and contrast the visual auditory and kinaesthetic submodalities of a *strong* belief (ie. something you believe with great conviction), and a *weak* belief (ie. something you don't have a strong opinion about one way or another) Note: a weak belief is NOT something you disagree with or feel negatively about, rather it is something you are *ambivalent* about.

2. Identify a *Limiting* Belief to Change
Identify the belief you want to change. Note the content and submodalities of this belief, and in particular its *location* in space, relative to where you picture the weak belief.

3. Move the Content of the Limiting Belief
Take the visual, auditory and kinaesthetic *content* of the limiting belief, and move it to the horizon and then in to the *same location* as the weak belief, and changing all the submodalities to be the same as those of the weak belief.

4. Build a New Belief
Make a picture frame for the new belief you want to have instead of the limiting belief, and build in appropriate visual, auditory and kinaesthetic content, using the same submodalities as those identified in your strong belief.

5. Install the New Belief
Take the picture of the new belief out to the horizon, then bring it back and lock it into position *at the location of the old limiting belief*. Repeat steps 3, 4 and 5 *quickly* six times.

6. Test and Futurepace
Test the change by thinking about the old limiting belief you used to hold. It should be experienced as a significant change. If not, repeat the exercise choosing another stronger 'strong' belief, and another weaker 'weak' belief.

To ensure you use the new belief in the appropriate contexts in future, think of some specific times in the future where you will want to have this new belief emerge spontaneously and unconsciously. Program in at least two or three future experiences to lock in your new belief.

CASE STUDY : Male Hockey Player
I used the above process to successfully change a young hockey player's negative belief that, "My hockey will never amount to anything". Such beliefs are common in players from all sports who are good players in their local leagues, but who keep getting overlooked for state or national selection. Consequently, these players can lose confidence, and quickly give up on their goals and even on their sport. Changing this negative belief was a top priority in helping him maintain his confidence and personal goals, without which no improvement happens in any player.

BUILDING POWERFUL, POSITIVE BELIEFS

In the above exercise, if you have trouble eliciting your own, or someone else's specific belief structure, use the question : "*How do you know?*" to help draw out the details. Eg. "*How do you know* ...... that you have a weak backhand; or that you're not a good public speaker; or that you don't play bunkers well; etc?" *Every* belief *must* be represented in terms of some visual, auditory and kinaesthetic information that you can identify - there is no other way to 'believe' something!

Having said that, often this information is below the usual conscious awareness of the individual - it's not something you normally think about, is it? Do recognise however, that the information is there - it has to be - it's just a matter of persisting with yourself or with the person you're working with to find it.

Also, note that it is important to first take the old belief out to the horizon before bringing it up into the same location of the weak belief - for some reason this works better than just trying to take it directly from one position to another!

To find a replacement belief ask "What would you rather believe?", or "What could you believe?"

The other thing that is vital in the above process is to have a positive replacement for the negative belief. Ask what would you rather believe, or what could you believe that would be more useful than the current negative limiting belief? Note that this may not be the exact opposite of the negative belief, because it would be too unrealistic. - eg. "I always slice" might become "I hit the fairway with 80% of my drives now", rather than "I never slice".

217

In this way, the selection of your desired beliefs becomes similar to the positive affirmation process I outlined in *Sportsmind* - and as with positive affirmations, for your new beliefs to imprint, they will want to adhere to some important principles.

I call these principles the 3 P's and a BEAN principles, and they are as follows:

The three P's stand for *Positive, Personal* and *Present Tense*. Make your desired belief a positive statement of what you want, rather than what you don't want. Secondly, include yourself in the belief - preferably experience yourself *associated* into the belief. For example, if I'm building a belief of being relaxed and comfortable speaking to an audience of 200 people, then I make an image of being there, looking out and seeing smiling faces and hearing loud applause.

> **The best way to acquire a skill is to act as if you have it now.**

Thirdly, your beliefs want to be framed either in the present, or within a very specified time frame - it's no use imagining being a certain way or having a particular skill or attribute 'sometime' in the future. The fastest way to acquire a skill is to act as if you have it now - mindful of course of safety issues, and working in achievable steps to achieve your goals. [I don't recommend imprinting a belief "I can skydive now" without proper training!]

The BEAN principles are *Behavioural, Emotional, Achievable,* and *Non-Comparative*. Behavioural means focus your attention in your belief building on the specific *behaviours* you need to achieve a particular goal.

For instance, rather than focusing on being a 'good' tennis player, golfer, cricketer, or whatever, identify the specific behaviours or skills that make a good player, and build that into your beliefs.

Emotional means make your beliefs compelling and generate strong feelings. Achievable means work in small steps to achieve big goals, as noted before. Non-comparative means build beliefs that are self focused, and not comparing self to others.

Finally, I've listed the following Champion beliefs as some that you may want to consider taking on, and building in yourself over the coming weeks. I've found them invaluable to my own performances in my sport, work and life!

POWER BELIEFS

* **What I say / speak becomes a reality.**
* **I have all the time I need now.**
* **I can do it. I can be, do and have whatever I aim for.**
* **I am a powerful person now. I am master of my destiny.**
* **Whatever I say after "I am ......" becomes true for me.**
* **Change and improvement in every situation is possible.**
* **I can change. Change is easy.**
* **Learning is easy and fun.**
* **Mistakes and 'failures' are useful feedback.**
* **Guilt is a useless emotion.**
* **My thoughts are powerful, and make things happen.**
* **I have all the resources I need to accomplish my goals.**
* **I am energetic and healthy now.**
* **I love my body and I treat it well.**
* **I deserve to do well. I am worthy of success now.**
* **It's not what others say to me, or think of me - it's what I say to myself, and think of myself that's important.**

*"You are a champion because you take
time for family and friends —
understanding the importance of
connecting with others."*

ABOUT
SPORTSMIND

THE SPORTSMIND VISION

When I wrote *Sportsmind* in 1993, I outlined a Vision to establish a network of interested people around the world and an education institute to provide Sports-NLP training. This worldwide network now has 3,000 sportspeople, coaches and sporting organisations. The *Sportsmind Institute for Human Performance Research*, established in 1996, provides two professional training courses to licence *Sportsmind* trainers; has a web site; provides a range of top quality books and audio tapes by leading NLP researchers; and produces *The Mental Edge* - a regular newsletter of Institute updates and new NLP techniques to improve your performance.

Over the next ten years our goal is to make *Sportsmind* a leading performance psychology provider for both the sporting and corporate world - and to establish a network of 1,000 *Sportsmind* performance consultants who can provide assistance for top athletes, sports clubs and corporations - worldwide. The people involved will have a practicing sports background (preferably still participating), have an interest in coaching, and be superb facilitators able to create learning environments which are challenging, enjoyable and directed at personal development for the highest good. To be part of this vision, you will complete both the *Sportsmind* Correspondence and NLP Practitioner courses.

If you're seriously interested in establishing a career in Sports-NLP performance psychology, then consider the opportunity involvement with Sportsmind provides.

To become part of the *Sportsmind* network, and to receive your FREE copy of *The Mental Edge*, please complete the reply card in the back of this book and return to:

SPORTSMIND   77 FLAXTON MILL RD
FLAXTON QLD 4560 Ph/Fax 07 5445 7994
email = jhodges@sportsmind.com.au
website = www.sportsmind.com.au

THE SPORTSMIND MISSION STATEMENT

 # To further the development of the Sportsmind Institute for Human Performance Research which function will be to :
- *produce high quality Sports-NLP books and tapes;*
- *promote Sportsmind training and Sports-NLP;*
- *train and support Sports-NLP trainers;*
- *research and disseminate new ideas and techniques;*
- *maintain standards of a professional association.*

 #   Sportsmind products and training courses will be widely sought after, acclaimed internationally, and have a positive effect on the lives of those they touch for their highest good. The Sportsmind training courses will generate an empowering atmosphere of learning, challenge and true personal growth.

 # The trainers involved with Sportsmind will have the utmost integrity and professionalism in their facilitation, and will continuously improve their own skills and knowledge through regular training, positive feedback and inspiration.

 # Sportsmind will attract all the human and financial resources for manifesting the vision, and will be prosperous - providing financial and inspirational support for those involved, and for other healing projects of worth in the wider community. Sportsmind will continue to evolve and grow.

REFERENCES & SUGGESTED READING

Andreas, S. and Faulkner, C.
1996 NLP The New Technology of Achievement Nicholas Brealey, London.

Andreas, C. and Andreas, S.
1989 Change Your Mind And Keep the Change Real People Press, Moab.
1989 Heart of the Mind Real People Press, Moab Utah.

Andreas, C. and Andreas, T.
1993 Core Transformations Real People Press, Moab Utah.

Bandler, R.
1985 Using Your Brain for a Change Meta Pubs, Cupertino California.
1993 Time for a Change Meta Pubs, Cupertino California.

Bandler, R. and Grinder, J.
1975 The Structure of Magic Science & Behaviour Books, Palo Alto.
1975 Patterns of the Hypnotic Techniques of Milton H. Erickson, M.D.
       Meta Publications, Cupertino California.
1979 Frogs Into Princes Real People Press, Moab Utah.
1980 Reframing Real People Press, Moab Utah.
1981 Tranceformations: Neuro-Linguistic Programming and the Structure of
       Hypnosis Real People Press, Moab Utah.

Castaneda, C.
1974 Tales of Power Penguin Books, Harmondsworth Middlesex.

Collingwood, C. and Collingwood, J.
1995 Personal Strategies for Life Inspiritive Pty. Ltd., Double Bay NSW.

Dilts, R.
1994 Effective Presentation Skills Meta Publications, Capitola CA.

Dilts, R., DeLozier, J., Bandler, R. and Grinder, J.
1980 NLP Volume 1 Meta Publications, Capitola CA.

Maltz, M.
1960 Psycho-cybernetics Prentice Hall, Englewood Cliffs New Jersey.

McClendon, T.
1980 NLP Practitioner Program McClendon & Assocs, St. Lucia Qld.
1981 Ericksonian Modelling Program McClendon & Assocs, St. Lucia Qld.

Robbins, A.
1986 Unlimited Power Simon & Shuster, New York.
1991 Awaken the Giant Within Simon & Shuster, New York.
1994 Giant Steps Simon & Shuster, New York.

Syer, J. and Connolly, C.
1984 Sporting Body, Sporting Mind Cambridge Uni Press, Cambridge.

More Praise for Jeffrey Hodges ......

"Jeffrey Hodges presented sports seminars for the Dept. Sport & Recreation on a number of occasions. To date, over 400 people have attended the seminars, but it is not so much the number of participants as the quality of the presentations which has been the standout feature of each lecture tour."
Lyn Larsen, Senior Recreation Officer, NSW Dept. Sport & Recreation.

"Congratulations! This is one of the most coherent models I've read in applied performance enhancement."
Geoff Dugan, Surfing and Aikido, NSW.

"Very useful. Clearly and powerfully presented at a practical level."
Heather McAlpine, personal trainer, NSW.

"Very well presented and informative. Related well to sports specific, pre-competition, competition, and post-competition preparation. Very useful."
Mark Waugh, P.E. Teacher, Qld.

"Very, very interesting and relevant to my coaching state league."
Alan Fairbanks, Netball, Victoria.

"Easy to read, well presented. Six week program is very useful."
Richard Thorpe, Karate, NSW.

" I am recommending Sportsmind to all my advanced pupils. "
A. Mackelvie, Level 2 Lawn Bowls Coach, Qld.

"Sportsmind is something I've been looking for for quite some time. Using the Sportsmind techniques I've improved my handicap by ten shots! It's a great book, and I would recommend it to anyone wanting to improve."
Joseph Caffo, golfer, NSW.

"I've been working with these techniques for over a year, and have many successful results and pleasure from using the Sportsmind approach".
Milo Bradley, Tennis Coach, Qld.

"Thankyou for the enormous help your workshops proved to be."
Ben Carruthers, Fencing, Vic.